The Cost of Quality Audit

A Management Toolkit to Drive Down the Cost of Errors, Inefficiency, Waste and Rework in Your Organisation

W. Jeffery Howard
The American Productivity & Quality Center

CSP

Cambridge Strategy Publications Ltd
Station Offices
Station Yard
Axminster EX13 5PF
United Kingdom

www.cambridgeaudits.com

Contents

Second Edition: 2010

ISBN 978-0-9559707-6-4

Part 1

The Cost of Quality Audit

This audit is structured in three parts. Part 1 examines the process of carrying out a Cost of Quality audit. Part 2 looks at the audit process itself and provides a framework that addresses some of the logistical and process requirements of conducting an audit. Part 3 comprises a series of questions based on the steps in Part 1. These questions are designed to help you plan and implement your audit in a straightforward and practical manner.

Introduction

Philip Crosby was one of the first people to bring the idea of the Cost of Quality to businesses outside Japan with his 1979 book .

Since then, the ideas on which he based his book have been developed into a complete management science. Total Quality Management (TQM), Customer Driven Quality and related Quality initiatives became commonplace in companies around the world. Inevitably, as the idea of Quality won acceptance, different 'gurus' and consultancy groups emerged and advocated different frameworks for implementing Total Quality.

In many countries the term 'Quality' has been superseded by the terms 'Excellence' or 'Business Excellence' and in some regions the philosophy of Quality has fragmented into approaches like Six Sigma, Best Practice and even Design Thinking. In Europe, the annual quality award has been renamed The EFQM Excellence Award while, in the USA, the prestigious Malcolm Baldrige Quality Award remains the only formal recognition of the performance excellence of U.S organisations given by the US President. But both awards and almost all business improvement models clearly retain the idea of Cost of Quality.

Unfortunately, some of these newer approaches to Quality have become so highly refined, and the rivalry between advocates of different routes to Quality has become so intense, that many organisations are now reluctant to embark on Quality improvement initiatives of any sort.

At the same time, a number of well-publicised Quality 'failures' have obscured the fact that Total Quality in some form has been the principal driver behind most of the companies that have achieved world-class standards of performance and customer service.

This Cost of Quality audit offers a quick and simple framework to help any organisation to go back to basics: to cut out waste and improve performance and profitability across the board. In short, it will show any organisation that it can improve Quality and save money at the same time.

How Measuring and Reducing the Cost of Quality Can Transform any Organisation

The compelling logic of improving Quality (for any organisation that is not already committed to doing so) is explained below. But the benefits of measuring and reducing the Cost of Quality in any organisation are clear and can be summarised here.

Running a regular Cost of Quality audit, and acting on its results, will:

- help to focus managers and staff on the way the organisation does business and the way it treats its customers.
- stimulate top management's interest in the financial and profit opportunities that could arise from a structured programme of Quality improvement.
- force senior management to recognise and acknowledge the crucial role that cross-functional business processes play.
- pinpoint the core business processes and operating areas that offer the most significant opportunities for improvement — in a way that no strictly financial audit ever can.
- act as an essential first step in any programme of company culture change, continuous improvement, Business Excellence, etc.
- help to identify levels of failure demand (that is, services like help-lines that exist largely or solely to receive complaints about, and try and put right, things the organisation did wrong previously).[1]
- describe Quality problems at least partly in monetary terms — which is a language that senior managers can easily understand and use to make decisions.
- help management to move away from budgets and targets that are based exclusively on historical performance. (A glass manufacturer, which had historically scrapped 15% of its output, set a scrap target rate of 13% for the coming year. On discovering that the total cost to the company of the existing 15% scrap level was over €3 million, it set a new target of 5% in the coming year).
- provide an overall index of the organisation's ability and effectiveness in getting key tasks and processes performed "right first time".
- reduce waste, delays, mistakes (and the direct and indirect costs associated with them) dramatically.
- improve communication (both internally and with suppliers) at all levels of the organisation.

[1]For a more detailed explanation of failure demand, see Seddon, 2008.

- help individual managers understand what happens in their department at an appropriate level of detail.
- increase customer satisfaction levels and improve customer retention levels.
- start to integrate useful, non-financial performance measures into the regular financial reporting round.
- help to prioritise future improvement projects and clarify future business strategy decisions right across the company.
- increase staff satisfaction levels and improve staff retention levels.
- improve overall business competitiveness, foster innovation, and reduce the time taken to develop new products or services.
- deliver results fast where they are most needed.
- increase overall company profits — often in a matter of weeks or a few months.

This is an impressive list — one which no organisation can afford to overlook. And, most important, it remains effectively unchallenged in spite of criticisms of the broader structure of Total Quality Management and other initiatives which often employ Cost of Quality measures as one of their key components.

How to Use this Self-Assessment Audit

This self-assessment audit draws on the experience of countless companies to present a simple and straightforward approach to auditing the Cost of Quality. No particular experience or training is required to run the audit — except for a basic understanding of business processes.

It sets out a clear, 14-step approach, with detailed examples and practical suggestions at every stage. It also provides all the "ammunition" necessary to convince a Board of Directors, the Chief Executive or the senior management team of the need to conduct a Cost of Quality audit, as well as the tools to act on the audit results.

It is designed to be read and used first by the Cost of Quality "champion", who will be ultimately responsible for the audit. Then it should be used as a handbook by the supervisory and audit teams that will actually administer the Cost of Quality measurement.

Throughout, examples and illustrations are drawn from different business sectors. This has been done to remind users that — although the term "company" is often used in these pages — the tools and techniques of a Cost of Quality audit apply to every organisation: for-profit or not-for-profit, manufacturing or service, publicly or privately owned. It should also help users to tailor the audit to the exact situation and circumstances of their organisation.

Where and When to Use a Cost of Quality Audit

The principal purpose of a Cost of Quality audit is to show, objectively, the real cost of doing things wrong, late or too often.

In a company that is embarking on a Total Quality or Business Improvement initiative, or already has one in place, the Cost of Quality audit will have a particular significance. But Cost of Quality is a measure that should be applied in any organisation, of any size and in any business sector. The results will always provide the incentive and the springboard for a programme of rapid and focused change.

Measured across a whole company, the Cost of Quality will normally lie between 20% and 40% of the company's annual turnover. This statistic is so shocking that managers often think they have misunderstood it. So it is worth restating. In simple terms, the cost of making mistakes and putting them right will be 20-40% of turnover. These figures have been documented time and time again.

- Ciba Corning Diagnostics estimated that its Cost of Quality was equal to 34% of turnover. Considering Corning was making $1.2bn a year, "non Quality" was costing a staggering $400 million.
- IBM's quality costs at one time were 30% of its manufacturing costs.
- At the UK's NatWest Bank, 25% of operating costs were found to be absorbed in the difference between the cost actually incurred in accomplishing a task and the cost of a "right first time" approach.[2]

The effect of showing these figures to any Board of Directors is likely to be so dramatic that a Cost of Quality audit is often used as the key argument to win top-level commitment to a Quality Improvement initiative. But ongoing Cost of Quality measurement is an integral part of Total Quality — and this audit can also be used to develop or fine-tune a continuing framework of Cost of Quality measures within a Quality or Business Improvement programme.

The good news is that world-class companies have been able to reduce their Cost of Quality to between 5% and 10% of annual turnover.

[2]All figures are taken from APQC research data.

Definitions

Before going any further, it is important to establish exactly what is meant by a Cost of Quality Audit.

Quality. The term Quality means different things to different people, and its meaning has evolved along with programmes to improve Quality. Before the dawn of the Quality era, many business leaders believed that Quality was an unmeasurable term which was somehow tied to increasing the number of features of any product and its overall level of luxuriousness. As the concept has been studied more thoroughly, however, it has become clear that even no-frills products and services can be of the highest Quality if they consistently meet the standards expected by their consumers given their price range and intended use. For example, a First Class seat on Singapore Airlines does not technically offer better Quality than an economy seat on a no-frills airline. Each is offering a different service to a different type of customer.

Thus, Quality has come to be seen as a highly measurable element; in fact, Quality results when the products and services offered by a company consistently meet measurable standards.

In the airline example above, Quality can be measured by the extent to which the flight (including price, departure time, check-in facilities, food, service, safety and time-keeping) meets the customer's expectations. Quality in this sense matters because the customer, if not satisfied, will fly with another airline next time.

Quality programmes have been embraced by managers because they accomplish two important goals. First, they provide customers with a more consistent product or service in less time. Second, they reduce the cost of making or providing that product or service by reducing waste, shortening production/delivery time, minimising the amount of inventory required and reducing the number of errors and complaints. While the savings resulting from these factors can be significant, the expense of not addressing them will continue as hidden costs if they are not rigorously monitored.

Cost. The Cost of Quality is the cost of everything a company does in trying to achieve 100% customer satisfaction PLUS the money it wastes whenever it fails to achieve that target.

This may seem an unnecessarily ambitious target. Many executives would be happy to accept 90% customer satisfaction. But this self-assessment guide will explain the unacceptable cost of even one dissatisfied customer, and running the audit will immediately confirm this.

Traditionally, the Cost of Quality has been broken down into three key elements: Prevention, Appraisal and Failure. A brief description of the types of cost falling within each area is given in Figure 2. A fuller listing will be found in Appendix A.

In the airline example, above, prevention costs would include: routine servicing and maintenance of the aircraft; provision of safety equipment and materials on board; staff training in areas like customer service, setting up and running a Quality system — everything the company spends to prevent errors, service failures or disasters happening.

Appraisal (or inspection) costs would include checking: that bolts had been tightened; that baggage had been appropriately routed; that the cabin had been cleaned — everything the company spends to check that routine prevention measures have been taken.

The combined cost of prevention and appraisal is often referred to as the cost of conformance. It includes all the costs deliberately incurred by the company in an effort to achieve Quality or customer satisfaction.

Failure costs would include the cost of: supplying a replacement aircraft if the scheduled aircraft was out of service or late; accommodating delayed passengers; finding and delivering wrongly-routed luggage; transporting passengers from a flight that had been overbooked; resolving customer complaints; issuing refunds; lost business resulting from bad publicity and dissatisfied customers.

Failure costs are often referred to as the cost of non-conformance or the cost of non-Quality. They include all the costs that the company unintentionally incurs in failing to achieve Quality or customer satisfaction. Failure costs are sometimes referred to as the cost of rework, but the term rework tends to leave out many of the intangible costs of failure.

FIGURE 1
THE COST OF QUALITY

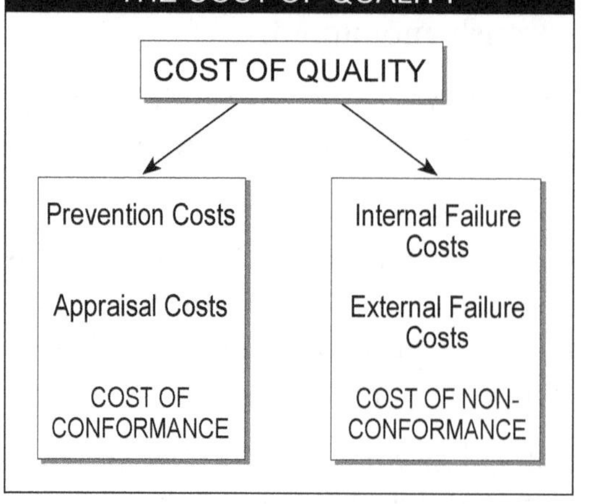

The Cost of Quality

Failure costs are usually broken down into the costs of "external failure" — those that directly affect the customer or consumer — and the costs of "internal failure" — which do not.

Audit. As explained below, it is normally prohibitively expensive and time-consuming to attempt a whole-company audit of the Cost of Quality. A series of individual business process audits will normally prove far more effective. For clarity, in the text of this book, the term "assessment" is sometimes used to describe these process audits and the term "audit team" is used to describe the group conducting the process audit or assessment. The term "Cost of Quality audit" is applied to the total picture which is then derived from these individual assessments and the term "Supervisory Team" is used to describe the group in charge of this overall process.

Understanding the Components of Cost of Quality

A quick review of any company will reveal that prevention costs are largely unavoidable — though the prevention processes involved can often be streamlined to work more effectively.

Note that any costs associated with running this Cost of Quality audit should be counted as a prevention cost. If anything, more should be spent on prevention to :

a) minimise the massive costs of product/service failure and

b) reduce the wasteful cost of inspection.

It will be seen that one of the objectives of the Cost of Quality audit must be to identify areas where the allocation of increased resources to prevention can deliver an immediate pay-back in terms of reduced inspection and failure costs.

Explaining this objective to staff will help to alleviate the main concern normally felt about a Cost of Quality exercise — that it is a cost-cutting exercise which will lead to job losses. In fact, by eliminating waste and unnecessary rework, as well as by reducing the cost of product/service failure, a Cost of Quality audit will free staff from the frustration of putting right mistakes and allow them to concentrate on value-added tasks — so generating increased profits and employment opportunities. At the same time, levels of employee satisfaction will increase, and staff turnover levels will begin to fall.

costs will generally form a very small proportion of the total (except in very high risk operations like nuclear power generation or health care). Nevertheless, better training, systems, staff morale and teamwork can often be used to reduce inspection costs still further.

costs will invariably form the largest single element of the Cost of Quality.

Figure 2, which lists a range of typical failure costs, will help explain how this comes about. (Some of the failure types listed in Figure 2 may appear to apply only to manufacturing companies. But close equivalents will also be found to exist for all service providers.)

TYPICAL FAILURE COSTS	
EXTERNAL FAILURE	INTERNAL FAILURE
Product recalls	Unrealistic deadlines
Wrong service provided	Lack of training
Product/service supplied late	Lack of planning for absence or illness
Repairing faulty products under guarantee	Computer downtime and disasters
Discounts/refunds/rework resulting from service failure	Poor hygiene
Redesigning faulty products	Failure to maintain production equipment
Incorrect labelling	Faulty documentation
Product liability	Poor time management
Litigation	Unnecessary meetings and reports
Order taken incorrectly	Scrap and waste materials
Storage and warehousing errors	Downtime because of a shortage of parts
Inadequate distribution vehicles	Retyping
Variation in materials	Faulty parts from external suppliers
	Overcapacity or undercapacity
	Unannounced schedule changes
	Poor filing
	Replacing staff
	Lack of consultation
	Progress chasing

Typical Failure Costs

A typical breakdown of the elements of the Cost of Quality is shown in Figure 3.

Running a Cost of Quality Audit

Many different approaches to running a Cost of Quality audit have been devised. For example, some enthusiasts claim that a true Cost of Quality audit will attempt to provide a definitive statement of all costs associated with Prevention, Appraisal and Failure across the whole organisation. Such an audit may eventually be useful or necessary. However, applying the Pareto principle, it can be generally assumed that some 20% of all Quality-related problems will account for around 80% of the Cost of Quality. For this reason, it may be counter-productive to spend valuable time in trying to identify or measure every single Quality cost. Better to focus on those areas where significant results can be achieved most quickly and most effectively.

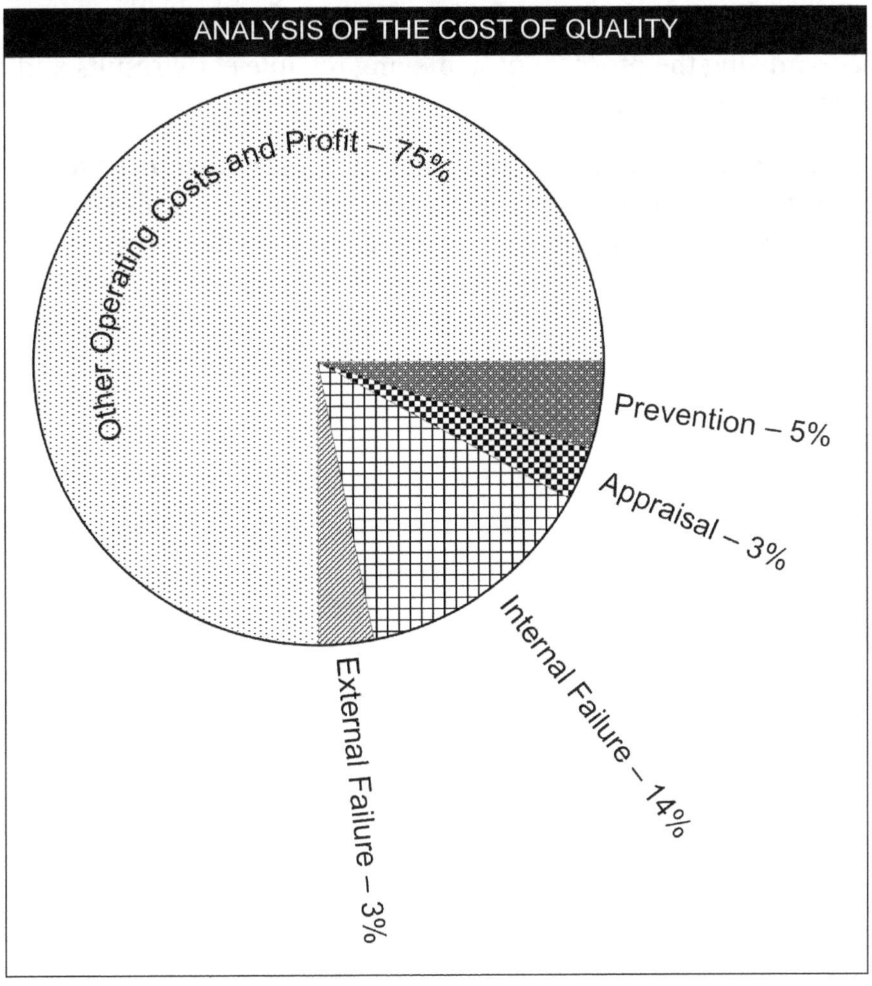

Analysis of the Cost of Quality

Some Cost of Quality audits have also attempted to define and measure costs in terms of the "cost to society" of failure or rework, or to use more conventional measures structured around Activity Based Costing (see **Step 14**).

However, this audit assumes that a series of Cost of Quality assessments will be undertaken to streamline core business processes rather than to provide a definitive, whole-company measure. Even in the context of a Total Quality programme it may be advisable to retain this same emphasis.

This process measurement approach has been shown to offer maximum business benefits without taking up valuable time in producing more comprehensive statistics that cannot be acted upon effectively.

These individual assessments must still be brought together into a single Cost of Quality audit, to permit comparisons between different business processes and to allow the development of an overall strategy that targets resources on areas that will benefit most from Quality improvement.

Note that starting out with this process measurement approach leaves the organisation free to move on to other audit refinements at a later date — without jeopardising the prospect of achieving reliable early results and cost and performance improvements.

As with all Cambridge Audits, the clear intention must be to use the audit results to identify signposts for change and opportunities for improvement, rather than to seek rigorously precise measurements for their own sake.

Steps in a Cost of Quality Audit

The following steps have proven most helpful in conducting successful Cost of Quality audits:

Step 1: Choosing the Supervisory Team

Applying simple rules to the selection of supervisory team members can make the difference between an unimaginative financial report and one that identifies clear and profitable ways forward for the organisation.

Step 2: Choosing the Processes to Be Audited

Understanding and selecting appropriate business processes is a key element in a successful audit. In some organisations, the act of focusing on business processes rather than on the traditional departmental structure may offer important benefits.

Step 3: Communicating the Audit Plan

The success of any Cost of Quality audit depends very largely on the willingness of all managers and staff to contribute freely and openly. Effectively communicating the audit's intentions will help to allay fears and win enthusiastic cooperation.

Step 4: Choosing the Audit Teams

The supervisory team selects the individual members of each process audit team, looking for people with the skills and experience to understand each business process well. Their work will ultimately decide the success of the whole audit.

Step 5: Defining Training Needs and Setting a Schedule

Not every organisation will need additional training in process management or Quality measures. For those that do, it is a straightforward process that will offer substantial advantages long after the audit has been completed.

Step 6: Defining and Mapping the Business Process

Here, individual audit teams lay the groundwork for their cost assessment, developing a clearer understanding of the process that they are auditing.

Step 7: Preparing to Calculate Quality Costs

The audit teams now begin to gather available data from in-house sources, which will help them allocate realistic costs within the main Quality cost categories.

Step 8: Determining the Causes of Quality Costs

The audit team here uses brainstorming techniques to determine bottlenecks and other sources of waste, delay and rework with their business process.

Step 9: Interviewing Staff

Each team member now briefs and interviews those involved in the process to get their input on likely and unsuspected Quality costs.

Step 10: Allocating Costs

The audit team uses agreed formulas and the information derived from interviews and management reports (Step 7) to allocate financial costs within each of the four main categories.

Step 11: Preparing the Audit Report

The audit reports condense and summarise the cost information that has been gathered, presenting the supervisory team with consistent data on which they can base their own conclusions.

Step 12: Preparing the Combined Audit Report

The supervisory team prepares a final Cost of Quality report which brings together the results of each assessment and focuses on opportunities for process improvement and cost reduction.

Step 13: Sharing the Findings and Taking Action

The combined audit report is presented to senior management and to all company staff as soon as possible. Top management must accept responsibility for problems that have caused Quality-related costs, but empower staff to identify ways of reducing these costs.

Step 14: Developing a Continuous Cycle of Audit and Improvement

The success of the Cost of Quality audit depends entirely on the extent to which it is just the first step in an ongoing cycle of assessment, measurement and Quality improvement.

Step 1

CHOOSING THE SUPERVISORY TEAM

The make-up of the supervisory team will vary considerably, depending on the size and complexity of the organisation. In addition to the general points on staffing the team in Part 2, there are a number of key points that specifically relate to a Cost of Quality audit which we can consider here:

Large companies should not be audited as a whole. Instead, individual business processes should be identified and assessed. In a large organisation, this may mean conducting as many as 30 separate Cost of Quality assessments.

Clearly, it is important to ensure consistency across all these assessments. To achieve this, key team members must be involved in the preparation and conduct of each of the assessments. However, in a large organisation, it will be unreasonably time-consuming for them to be involved at every stage of each assessment. In a smaller organisation, it may be possible for the supervisory team to conduct some or all of the audits, thereby removing the need for separate audit teams.

It is usually advisable to form a steering committee (here called the "supervisory team"). This will normally consist of three people: the team leader — the manager or director in overall charge of the Cost of Quality audit; a senior member of the finance or accounts department; a member of the Training/ Personnel/Human Resources team or a senior administrative assistant.

The team leader will probably be the Total Quality or Business Improvement manager or director, or any other senior company officer from outside the finance or accounts department. Their seniority should reflect the importance that the company attaches to the results of this audit, and demonstrate top management commitment to the project. In any case, the team leader should have the experience and ability to think widely about issues across the whole company, and be able to insist on attention to detail, without becoming immersed in the minutiae of each assessment.

The presence of the accountant on the team is a reminder that the Cost of Quality audit is, in part, a genuine financial audit. The accountant will also be able to ensure that consistent measures are used in each assessment and that the dangers of double-counting are minimised.

The third team member should be closely involved with all aspects of the company's work and know many of the individuals on each audit team. This person should normally be made responsible for training the members of each audit team and ensuring that each team keeps to established schedules and produces the required report in an appropriate format.

Step 1 Summary: *Select the three members of the supervisory team, which must include a representative from the Accounts/Finance function.*

Step 2

Choosing the Processes to Be Audited

The supervisory team's first task — normally in conjunction with the CEO or the management team as a whole — is to decide the scope of the Cost of Quality audit. Here it should be stressed that the role of the audit will not normally be to come up with a definitive statement of Quality costs across the whole organisation (see Introduction). In fact, such an exercise could be counter-productive — much time will be wasted trying to identify hidden, but insignificant, costs and itemise them to the finest degree.

Since one purpose of the audit will be to focus attention on the company's core business processes, considerable care should be taken in fixing the audit's scope.

Many companies will have already mapped their core business processes, and selecting processes to be audited will be relatively easy. For those that have not done so, it will be more time-consuming. But, for this group, the Cost of Quality audit will be doubly valuable because of the additional insights into the working of the organisation that will be found.

Figure 4 gives some additional information on core business processes for newcomers to this approach, which will rapidly introduce the tools and techniques of business process mapping.

To ensure that the Cost of Quality audit is taken seriously by staff and managers, processes should be chosen which, together, touch or cross every single site, department, operation or team in the organisation. Otherwise, the audit runs the risk of alienating employees who are not in any way involved in it. Normally, it will be beneficial if most of the processes chosen are ones that end with the customer. However, it will be necessary to include a few internal processes (such as choosing, ordering and distributing office supplies, or identifying staffing requirements, advertising, interviewing and appointing new members of staff).

The objective of including every department and significant work group will define how many processes are chosen for assessment. This may be as few as 5 or 6, or as many as 30. If a very large number of processes is identified, it may be appropriate to make the first round of assessments a pilot scheme and restrict the audit to one site or division.

Equally, if the company is unfamiliar with business process management, it may also be appropriate to limit the scope of the first audit. In the long-run, it will be more effective to set limited, but achievable, targets for the audit.

It is also advisable to limit the scope of individual processes to manageable proportions. For example, in a restaurant, the process of feeding the customer could be taken to begin with deciding next week's menu and to end with paying for the meal. But the assessment will be easier to conduct — and will involve fewer staff — if the process is taken to start at the point where the customer places an order, and to finish when the correct meal is served at the optimum temperature to the right customer at an agreed interval after the order was placed.

CORE BUSINESS PROCESSES

In most cases, business processes will run horizontally across an organisation, where typical departments and reporting structures run vertically from top to bottom of the company. Processes typically represent the way the company actually does business far more accurately than a departmental structure.

Historically, process analysis began on the production line where, for example, a number of parts are bolted together to form a washing machine or motor vehicle. But the same principles can be applied to any part of a manufacturing or service operation:

- The invoicing process: Issuing invoices, receiving payments, checking them, banking them, and reporting them is an example of a business process that (unusually) is confined to just one department.
- The order/customer generation process: The process of generating new orders or customers may start in the marketing department, move through the sales or promotion department, and be completed in the department that processes online orders.
- In a bank, the process of opening a new account or completing a foreign currency transaction is likely to involve credit checking, inputs from several departments and even from different branches.
- In a retail outlet, the process of choosing, specifying, ordering, stocking and replenishing goods can involve a wide range of staff and computer systems at different sites.

Focusing on these core processes will help to concentrate attention on the customer (for whose benefit the process exists) rather than on the reporting systems and administrative requirements of the company (which do not add value, generate customers or earn profits — and may often slow down the process so much that the customer is tempted to go elsewhere).

Core Business Processes

For each business process to be assessed, the supervisory team should simply define the starting-point and finishing-point for the process. This will ensure that the processes to be assessed do not overlap. Individual audit teams should be given complete freedom to decide what tasks to include in the process.

Almost invariably, it will be found that the scope of the process and the "inputs" considered will increase as the assessment team continues its work.

Step 2 Summary:

Step 3

Communicating the Audit Plan

Before choosing or briefing the audit teams, the supervisory team must be absolutely clear what it wishes to achieve in conducting the audit. This aim should be condensed into an audit mission statement which encapsulates the chief purposes of the audit. The mission statement may include references to any or all of the following:

- The wish to better understand the key business processes which drive the company's performance and profitability.
- The wish to identify specific Quality cost improvement projects which will rapidly deliver tangible benefits to the company and its staff.
- The intention — within the processes being assessed — to identify and reduce waste, rework and the cost of product failure and service breakdown, wherever they are found.
- The hope that, by cutting down on waste, rework and failure, staff will be able to concentrate on more productive, rewarding and enjoyable work.
- An undertaking that no blame will attached to any individual for costs uncovered by the audit (see Figure 5).
- If possible, an undertaking that no jobs will be lost as a result of any savings that may be made following the audit and its recommendations (see Figure 5).

Note that it is not suggested that the audit should set out to develop a definitive Cost of Quality measure across the whole company. Limiting the objective to identifying those processes where substantial improvements can be made will obviously affect the way that the individual audit teams work. This approach of identifying high-cost problems reduces the time-consuming need to identify and quantify every single Quality Cost.

Limiting the objective will also have important implications for the way staff perceive the audit. If the audit tries to offer a definitive statement of costs, critics will probably be quick to identify oversights or errors. This may discredit the entire audit. Better to recognise in advance that the audit is accurate only to within ±15%. This will defuse many criticisms.

OVERCOMING RESISTANCE TO COST OF QUALITY AUDITING		
It is important to be aware that Quality costing frequently raises fears, objections and resistance among managers and staff at all levels. These objections need to be anticipated and dealt with early on in the audit cycle. It may help to refer to these fears in the audit mission statement, but one-to-one discussion, explanation and reassurance will often also be necessary. The three main objections that are likely to be encountered before and during a Cost of Quality audit are as follows:		
THE THREE-DAY WONDER	DON'T BLAME ME	THE "COST CUTTING" SYNDROME
In companies that have seen change and improvement initiatives come and go, there may well be scepticism about the merits of a Cost of Quality audit and about the likelihood of it delivering any of the results which have been promised. Here it is important to stress that Quality Costing is not a theory or a fad. The cost of getting things wrong is as real and tangible a cost as the electricity bill. The only difference is that conventional accounting procedures do not report this cost. Identifying and measuring this cost is the first, inevitable step on the way to reducing that cost. Whether the workforce believes that any or all of the money saved by reducing the Cost of Quality will be invested in training, research, and technology will depend on the company culture and the previous record of the management team. If people do not believe that they will see any direct benefit from reducing the Cost of Quality, it may be appropriate to include specific assurances in the mission statement.	Many people may feel threatened by the idea of a Cost of Quality audit — particularly managers and staff who have held their jobs for a considerable time, or who are hoping to win promotion or pay increases in the near future. Not unnaturally, they will fear that the audit may uncover particularly high costs in an area or process for which they are responsible. Once again, it will be important to stress in the mission statement that Quality costs are due to the company's own systems. The company should clearly acknowledge that it is systemic faults rather than faults or failings with individuals that generate Quality costs and cause inefficiency. Make it clear that no blame will be attached to any individual for costs that are identified during the audit — though they will be responsible for implementing changes to which they have agreed as a result of the audit.	"Downsizing" exercises in many companies have led to a fear that any move to cut costs will automatically lead to job losses. Many people will, therefore, fear that the hidden agenda is to identify areas where the size of the workforce could be cut. In fact, nothing could be further from the truth, since it will be failure cost that is the principal target for any subsequent cost reductions. Indeed, it should be explained that identifying and reducing the Cost of Quality will actually reduce the likelihood of job losses since a loss-making company may be able to climb back into profit through a concerted attempt to reduce Quality costs. This should be clear to anyone who properly understands the components of Cost of Quality and the nature of the audit. It is a reminder of the need for everyone to be absolutely clear about the purpose of the audit.

Figure 5: Overcoming Resistance to Cost of Quality Auditing

Finally, if, as it should be, the Cost of Quality audit is repeated at regular intervals to measure improvement, it is more likely to fall into disuse if it is unduly time-consuming.

The mission statement has three main purposes:

- It should be presented to the Board of Directors or the senior management team to help clarify the team's intentions and the results that can be expected from the audit.
- It should be referred to by the supervisory team, especially in preparing the final report.
- It should be used as the basis for all staff and audit team briefings to ensure a consistency of purpose and to help clear-up potential misunderstandings.

(For further information and advice on this step, see **Part 2: the Audit Process**).

Step 3 Summary: *The supervisory team must establish its objectives and develop an appropriate mission statement.*

Step 4

CHOOSING THE AUDIT TEAMS

For each process to be assessed, an audit team should be chosen. Normally, there should be 3-5 people on each team. The actual number will be decided by the number of different departments through which the process flows — it is essential that each department is represented on the audit team if the results are to win widespread acceptance.

Again, it is important that each audit team member has a good understanding of the process involved. Equally, they must not have obvious vested interests in maintaining the status quo. For example, a key department manager may be reluctant to reveal waste or inefficiency for fear that this may put promotion opportunities at risk.

For these reasons, younger department members may be the most suitable, but they will typically need to have been with the company for at least two years in order to be familiar with its operation overall. (Here it may be helpful to ask individual department managers or team leaders to nominate an enthusiastic and communicative member of staff to represent them on the assessment team.)

Depending on the make-up of each audit team, it may also be helpful to nominate a different member of the finance or accounts department to sit on each team. This will help to minimise the time needed to train non-financial staff in the fundamentals of accounting. It will also help to avoid audit teams spending valuable time measuring or calculating costs (like Quality Assurance staffing costs) which may already be well known to the accounts or finance department. Finally, accounts staff will be the most knowledgeable about the assumptions and guidelines used in allocating costs to different accounts or expenditure categories.

If the number of individual process audits to be run is very few, the supervisory team may be closely involved at almost every stage of each assessment. If the number is large, the supervisory team will simply be responsible for introducing each audit team to its task, monitoring progress, assisting with the preparation of the assessment results, and producing the final report.

Step 4 Summary:

Step 5

Defining Training/Development Needs and Setting a Schedule

Once the mission statement has been agreed and the audit teams have been chosen, the supervisory team will need to consider the requirement for additional training in understanding and assessing business processes and the Cost of Quality. In many organisations that already focus on processes, this will not be necessary. But, for others, a range of materials now exists to help understand, monitor and train staff in process management.

The necessary training for each audit team should probably take no more than a day. This will include exercises, discussion groups and break-out sessions to test the applications of the concepts learned and to focus on applying the general rules to the specific conditions of the organisation or process under discussion.

A key component of any training that may be deemed necessary will be a proper understanding of the concept of the internal customer. Audit team members may easily overlook Quality costs if they focus only on the requirements of the end-user of the product or service. Quality Costs, particularly costs of internal failure, will apply predominantly to a failure to supply information, goods or services as required by an internal customer. (This internal customer will normally be the next person or group in the process chain).

To help clarify training needs, to ensure that a consistent message is communicated to all audit teams, and to ensure that unreasonable demands are not placed on these teams, it may be advisable for the supervisory team to conduct a limited process audit itself. This should be confined to an internal process which is well-known to all the team members and which does not require the involvement of other staff. (Identifying and providing training, or hiring new employees are both suitable candidates for this assessment.) The results of this "demonstration audit" need not be published. The purpose of conducting the audit is to familiarise the supervisory team with some of the problems that will subsequently be faced by the audit teams.

Having defined the mission statement and agreed training needs, the supervisory team must agree a schedule. 2-3 months will normally be sufficient. All the assessments should be run concurrently. The supervisory team will also need to outline the likely number of audit team meetings required, decide how often the audit teams should report their progress, and agree a structure for the final report to be submitted by each audit team. (See Step 11 on reporting assessment results).

Finally, the whole audit scheme must be presented to the company. It is important that all members of staff are briefed, even those who will not be directly involved in any of the assessments. This will help to avoid misguided rumours spreading about the intentions of the supervisory team. In a large organisation this will need to be done via individual managers, who will need to be fully briefed first.

Wherever possible, the CEO or a senior colleague should be present at staff briefings. It is essential that everyone understands that a Cost of Quality audit is quite unlike a standard financial audit. The Cost of Quality audit is designed to give everyone involved a completely new picture of the organisation. It will reveal dramatic and unexpected statistics but, at the same time, uncover opportunities for the company to revolutionise the whole way that it does business. Liberal use may be made of relevant figures — for example, that ITT Europe identified its Cost of Quality at over $500 million when it first conducted an audit. But, be careful not to refer to Cost of Quality as a percentage of turnover at this stage. Audit team members should be encouraged to include all the costs they can think of, but not feel they have to reach a magic target of 20% or 30% in order to demonstrate that their particular assessment has been a successful one.

Step 5 Summary: *The supervisory team must ensure that all staff fully understand the purpose of the audit and that all those working on assessment teams are fully familiar with business process mapping and the concept of the internal customer. Training must be provided where necessary.*

Step 6

Defining and Mapping the Business Process

Having chosen a team leader to assign tasks and monitor progress, each audit team is now ready to begin work.

The audit team's first task, which should not be hurried, is to define and then map the business process in question. It is assumed that all the team members are closely involved in the process and that, between them, they are familiar with almost every stage of the process. Process mapping should not, therefore, require additional research. Rather, it will be concerned with defining the parameters of the process, the "inputs" to be included, and areas to be excluded.

At this stage, the intention should be to make the process definition as comprehensive as possible. Subsequently, the definition may be refined to focus attention on the core process rather than on particular "inputs" which may have grown more complex than the core process itself.

The sample process flow map shown in Figure 6 uses conventional process mapping symbols. It charts part of the process of recruiting a new staff member to fill a job vacancy. It will be clear from the process map that the central process of filling the vacancy is in danger of being overwhelmed by the problems associated with getting permissions, authorisation and approvals at each stage. (Process mapping software to facilitate the creation of the flow maps is readily available and easily used.)

For clarity of presentation, it will be necessary to abbreviate the process flow map (see Figure 7). This truncated map should then be submitted to the supervisory team. At this stage the supervisory team should not seek to interfere with, or challenge, the process map (unless it has obviously overlooked key process steps). Rather, the supervisory team should compare the maps submitted by each of the Audit teams to ensure that there is no overlap between the different processes being assessed.

While the audit team will present the abbreviated process map to the supervisory team, it is important to retain a copy of the fuller version for the assessment itself, since many of the potential Quality costs will inevitably lie in those areas of the map that have been left out. This fuller map will also be an essential source of reference in all future assessments in the Cost of Quality audit cycle.

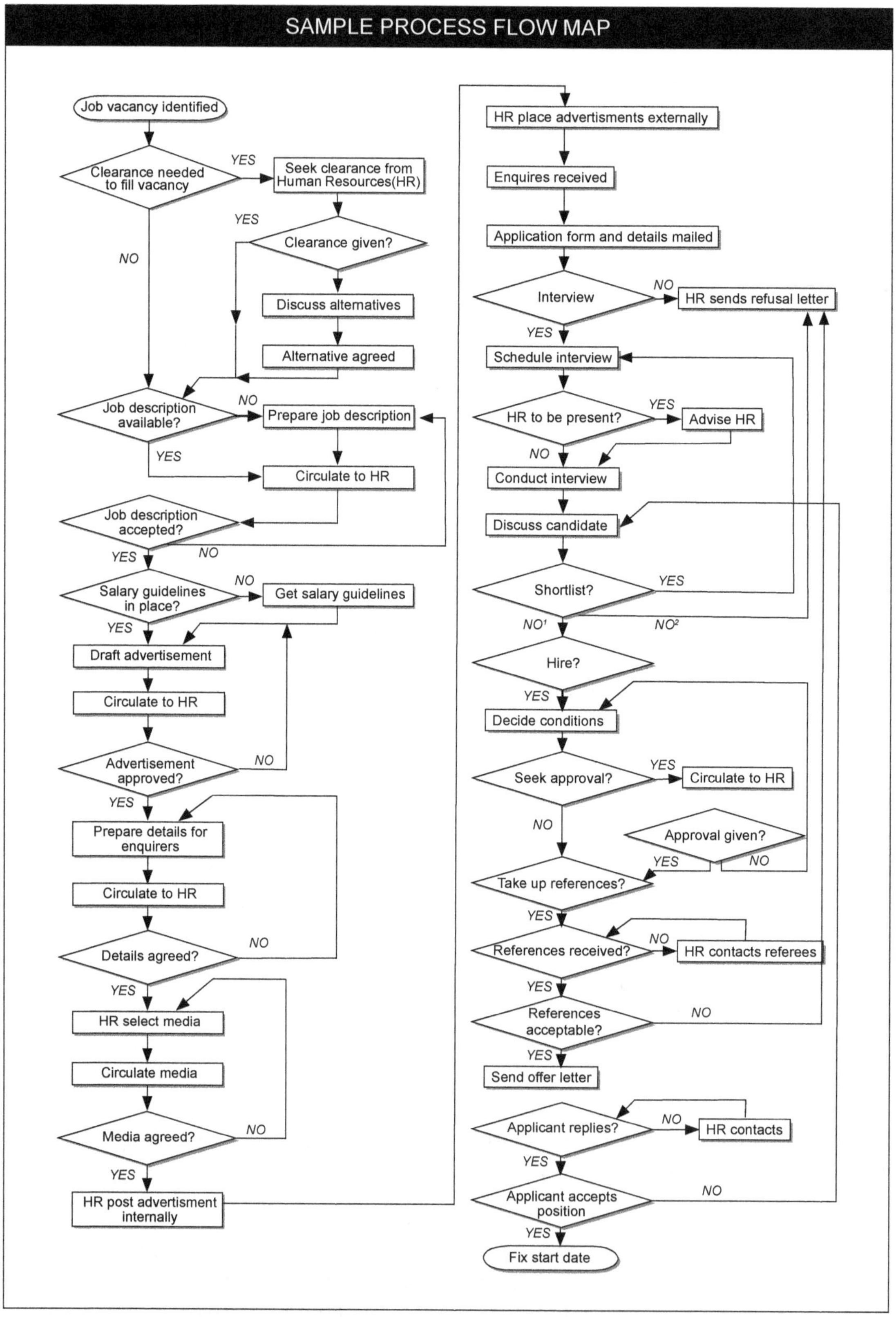

Figure 6: Sample Process Flow Map

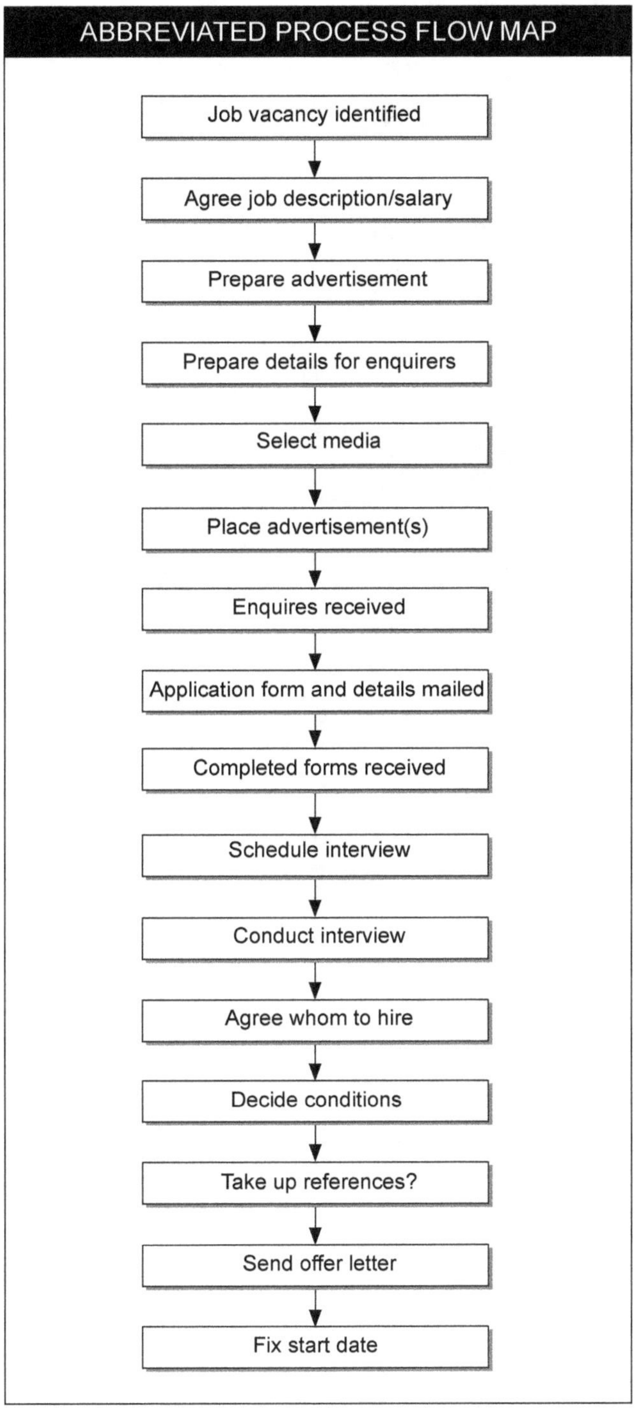

Figure 7: Abbreviated Process Flow Map

Step 6 Summary: *The audit team prepares a detailed process flow map, with an abbreviated version for scrutiny by the supervisory team.*

Step 7

Preparing to Calculate Quality Costs

In Step 8 (below) the audit team will begin to break down Quality costs into time-related costs, "out-of-pocket" costs relating to materials and supplies, and other intangible costs.

As preparation for the analysis of time-related costs, the audit team should prepare a list of all the staff involved in any way at every stage of the process. (Additional staff members may be identified as involved in the process during Step 9 — they can simply be added to the list at that time). This staff listing will help to ensure that all of the time costs associated with the Cost of Quality are properly assessed.

These staff should be categorised in bands (e.g. senior manager, manager, staff) which approximate to wage/salary scales. This framework will be used to convert time spent on Quality-related activities into cash amounts.

Once this has been done, the audit team — with particular input from the accounts department representative — must calculate the average burden rate for each group of employees.

The burden rate is the cost of company-provided benefits, including health insurance, unemployment insurance, vacation time, etc. This is usually described in terms of one percentage figure for all employees, or two different figures if there is a significantly different burden rate for the highest paid people in the organisation as compared to the lowest paid. The burden rate usually runs between 15% and 30% of wages. All time costs calculated during the course of the audit should be increased by this percentage, since it represents additional savings that will accrue if the activities associated with the Cost of Quality are not performed.

Step 7 Summary: *The audit team must calculate appropriate multiples to allow the conversion of time-related Quality costs into a monetary equivalent.*

Step 8

Determining the Causes of Quality Costs

Now that the process map has been approved, the audit team should break down the map into a number of component parts (perhaps four or five) which can be labelled or colour coded. The team will then use modified brainstorming techniques to identify as many factors as possible that contribute to Prevention, Appraisal and Failure costs. If the audit team feels that its understanding of particular process stages is limited, it may want to call in additional members of staff to join in the brainstorming session. (Involving other staff members at this stage has also been shown to be an effective way of winning the support of employees who are otherwise sceptical or critical of the audit).

As a general rule, it is more important to list all relevant cost areas than to categorise them with absolute accuracy. Equally, it is more important to spend time on areas that contribute substantially to the Cost of Quality than on areas that contribute only marginally. For example, it may be debated how much, if any, of the cost of customer surveys and questionnaires should be allocated as a Cost of Quality, and how much is a genuine market research process. Should they be classified as an inspection cost or as the unavoidable result of product/service failure? There is no definitive answer and — since their cost will be relatively low in most companies — it is not normally worth wasting time trying to find one.

The brainstorming workshop should last two to three hours. If this proves insufficient, separate workshops can be run to look at the different process components previously identified and coded. The brainstorming workshop should be structured in four phases as follows:

Phase 1

Before the workshop, each participant should be asked to complete a condensed process self-assessment form (Figure 8). These sheets can be completed online and printed out for use in meetings or they can be completed by hand. Heading this sheet "How time and money is wasted" will serve as a reminder of the real purpose of the exercise for people who are perhaps confused or daunted by the concepts of Cost of Quality. A copy of the process map should be attached to the worksheet. It will also be useful to preface this worksheet with a short definition of the terms Prevention, Appraisal and Failure, along with examples of each one (the typical cost types listed under each category in Appendix A will be useful here). It must be stressed that no attempt should be made at this stage to attach any cost estimates to the activities that are identified.

Phase 2

At the workshop, team members should take turns to call out one activity from their worksheet, which is then written up in the appropriate category. When this has been completed, members will probably have new suggestions as a result of hearing the activities that other team members have identified. These also should be written up. Up to this point, no discussion or evaluation of any of the activities should be allowed.

Phase 3

This phase of the workshop should be devoted to grouping and ordering the suggested areas and activities into Prevention, Appraisal, Internal Failure and External Failure costs, amending or removing any that are generally agreed to be inappropriate or irrelevant.

CONDENSED PROCESS SELF-ASSESSMENT FORM

HOW TIME AND MONEY IS WASTED

For the process (or process segments) shown on the attached process map, list as many jobs or activities as you can which fall into the following categories (if you are not sure which category they belong to, list them separately at the end).

(allow at least half a page for each category)

Prevention:

Appraisal or inspection:

External failure or rework:

Internal failure or rework:

Figure 8: Condensed Process Self-Assessment Form

It is important at this phase to ensure that built-in costs (often called yield allowances) are not overlooked. For example, it is company policy in many printing firms to print and deliver up to 10% more than the quantity ordered by the customer. This is done to avoid the potentially heavy cost of reprinting if the exact quantity is printed and a handful of faulty copies are found. Because this yield allowance is established company policy and built into all estimates and production costs, it may not be spotted as a Cost of Quality.

The outcome of this session should be a listing, similar in scope to that shown in Appendix A, but "personalised" to suit the business process under discussion.

Phase 4

Towards the end of the session, in Phase 4, team members should consider the Cost of Quality factors that they have identified in another way. Within each of the four categories (Prevention, Appraisal, Internal Failure, External Failure) costs will be found to fall into three types:

Tangible or out-of-pocket expenses:

In a manufacturing process, these will include:

- raw materials or parts which are rejected, damaged or otherwise not used.
- finished and part-finished goods which are thrown away because they do not conform to requirements in some way.

In a service or administrative process, these will include:

- printed materials, stationery and other outputs, which cannot be used.
- goods and services which have been ordered in error or in excess and which are, therefore, wasted or not used.

Out-of-pocket expenses will also include all other measurable costs relating to warranties, refunds, safety materials and so on.

Time:

This will include time spent in working on or with goods and services that are wasted or never used, as well as time spent putting right, correcting or repairing damage, errors or product and service failures, and time spent "rebuilding" relationships with customers that have been damaged as a result of delay or the provision of faulty goods and services.

Other intangible costs:

These costs will principally include "opportunity costs", which are one of the most contentious areas of Quality costing. Opportunity costs relate almost exclusively to external failure and can include, for example, the potential profit which could have been earned by staff during the time that they were "wasting" time as defined above.

For example, in a vehicle service station, mechanics might spend, on average, 26 man-hours per week awaiting deliveries of parts or putting right faults that were not fully resolved in a previous service. The Quality cost can be calculated in two ways:

a) as a time-related cost, which multiplies hourly wage plus the burden rate (Step 7) by 26 — the number of hours wasted.

b) as an opportunity cost, which shows the profit (sales minus wages, burden rate and other overheads) that could have been earned in those 26 hours.

As a rule, the second approach is more complicated, more time-consuming and more prone to error. And the result of both calculations will not normally be significantly different. It is, therefore, suggested that approach a) be used.

Intangible costs will also include the cost of alienating customers and so losing their future custom and the custom (or potential future custom) of associate companies (in a business-to-business environment) or their families and friends (in a consumer market). Associated with this, there will normally be the cost in sales, marketing and promotion terms of replacing a lost customer.

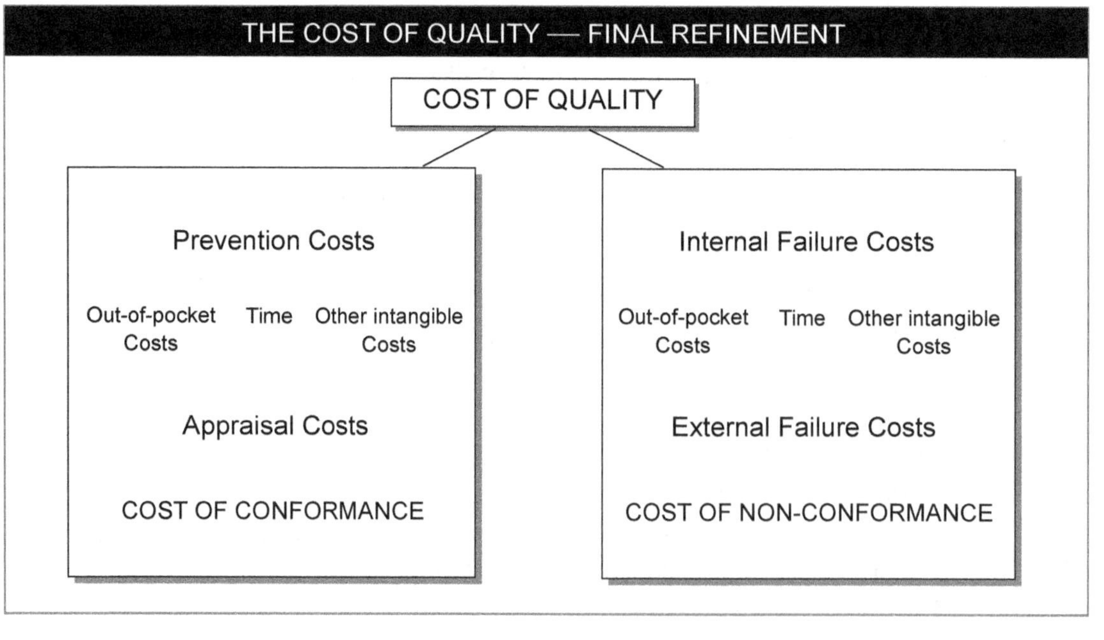

Figure 9: The Cost of Quality – Final Refinement

Allocating the cost areas that have previously been identified into one or other of these types will help to reveal costs that might otherwise have been missed. It will also provide a useful focus during the staff interviews (Step 9).

Appendix B shows the categories of Internal Failure and External Failure allocated as tangible, time-related and intangible. Note that, in some categories, costs may fall into more than one of these types.

This final refinement of the different elements of the Cost of Quality is shown in Figure 9.

Step 8 Summary: *The audit team uses a brainstorming workshop to identify and categorise potential Quality-related costs associated with the process under review.*

Step 9

Interviewing Staff

The members of the audit team cannot be expected to know, or understand fully, exactly how each individual working on any aspect of the business process spends their time. Equally, many tangible/out-of-pocket costs which should be included in the assessment may normally be hidden from view. If conventional financial audits have not recognised these costs, it will be necessary to ask the staff involved to help identify them.

The audit team must now agree an interviewing procedure and schedule in order to gather this information.

First, decide whether all staff associated with the process can be interviewed. If this would be impracticable, identify appropriate representatives from each department or work group who could be interviewed. It may be helpful in some cases to decide to interview a small group of three or four staff. This will have the advantage that the interviewees may give each other ideas and provoke lateral thinking on possible Quality costs, as well as being able to cross check each other's estimates of time spent on particular activities. The group interview approach is particularly helpful where the interviewer does not have a close working knowledge of the process stage under review.

Each audit team member should now be given responsibility for interviewing their share of staff members. Depending on the number of issues to be covered and the number of people present, the interview may last from one to three hours.

The interview itself falls into five separate phases.

In **Phase 1**, give a brief explanation of the aims of the interview and the terms which are being used. It is not necessary for the interviewee to understand the fine distinctions between different categories of Quality costs. The interviewer will be responsible for allocating costs to the relevant category.

In the course of this explanation, which may last for 10 or 15 minutes, the interviewer should give examples of the sort of costs that are being identified (see Figure 2 and Appendix A).

In **Phase 2**, ask the interviewee(s) to describe the major and minor functions of their job/department/work group. Record their comments on a simple form.

In **Phase 3**, have the group identify the number of people in the department/

work group and agree on how many fall into each of the three or four salary levels identified in Step 7. Record this information — it will be used to convert time spent on Quality-related issues into a financial equivalent.

Phase 4: For each of the major activities identified in Phase 2, go through the list of causes identified by the audit team in audit Step 8 and illustrated in Appendix B. Ask the interviewee(s) to estimate:

- the amounts of services and materials (tangible costs) associated with each item.
- the amount of time spent by different people in the department on the various activities.

It is essential, for each estimate, to record the period to which it relates — day, week, month, etc. The periods quoted do not need to be consistent, but must be known so that the subsequent financial calculation can be made accurately.

Record the answers on a Cost of Quality survey sheet (see Figure 10). Note that the interviewee(s) are not asked to convert the materials/time into a financial cost. This is done by the audit team (Step 10). However, it is necessary to ask the interviewee(s) to break down the time estimate into the salary levels already agreed — this will allow an accurate conversion into financial cost.

SAMPLE COST OF QUALITY SURVEY SHEET

Process: Order Fulfilment		*Date:* 26 April 2011		
Work Group: Telesales		*Interviewer:* AJR		
ACTIVITY	EXPENSES	TIME BAND 1	BAND 2	BAND 3
Handling complaints	Call charges:	1 hr/week a	4 hrs/week a	28 hrs/week a
(incoming calls and	21 hrs/week standard	4 hrs/week b	6 hrs/week b	12 hrs/week b
calling customers	12 hrs/week Freephone	2 hrs/week c		
who have written	Training costs			4 hrs/month d
to complain)				
	COMMENTS	COMMENTS		
	No other significant materials	a = time on telephone		
	used. See accounts for cost	b = preparation/paperwork relating to calls		
	of trainer (external consultant)	c = meetings		
	[check call reports for % of	d = training		
	customers lost]			

Figure 10: Sample Cost of Quality Survey Sheet

Expect to find that, on average, about 10 to 50% of the group's time will be spent on Cost of Quality activity, with the majority of their time being spent on other work. The activity of some group members, such as an inspector, will be almost totally devoted to Quality.

Throughout the meeting, ask for, and record, comments from the interviewee(s) about the causes of why large blocks of time are spent on Quality-related activities. These areas will suggest ideas for improvement projects in the analysis phase of the audit. It is also an important stage in convincing staff that the assessment is not just another "numbers exercise", but a genuine opportunity to change their jobs and the way they work — with substantial input from themselves.

In **Phase 5**, encourage the interviewee(s) to think of as many other Prevention and Appraisal activities, as well as other causes of failure and rework — apart from those listed. Again, seek estimates of tangible and time-related costs for each new activity identified.

Problems at the interview stage

Interviewees may be uncertain about how much time is spent on a particular activity. In this case, the activity should be discussed until a rough estimate can be made.

- Interviewees may be afraid to reveal figures that might suggest incompetence or complacency on their part or on the part of their manager. Reassure them by telling them figures that have been found in other (unnamed) departments and by reminding them that no blame will be attached to any individual, however high the costs of wasted time or materials that they report. At the same time, be aware that some interviewees may offer exaggerated estimates in order to highlight incompetence that they perceive in their managers or in company systems.
- Interviewees may be confused by the separation of costs into Prevention, Appraisal and Failure. This is not important. The interviewer or audit team can subsequently reorder activities as appropriate.

Step 9 Summary: *Each member of the audit team interviews representatives from departments / work groups with a significant input into the process. A five-phase interview technique is used to collect consistent data.*

Step 10

ALLOCATING COSTS

Once the interviews have all been completed, the audit team will begin to allocate costs to each of the activities that it has identified.

First, the finance/accounts representative on the team should identify any areas where costs have already been calculated or are available. These may include payroll breakdowns, production expense or scrap reports, travel expenses claims, and repair and replacement cost reports. These costs (in the case of staff costs, normally relating to prevention and appraisal personnel) should then be obtained.

In many cases, accounts will have to be divided between normal activity and Quality-related activity. It will often be necessary to interview a department manager for suggestions on how to make this apportionment. For example, express and courier mail and shipment costs may be partially due to normal activity and partially due to emergencies caused by internal failure. The accounts will almost certainly not reveal this distinction.

Do not overlook other reports or management information sources which may record how often a failure occurs or an assessment activity occurs, but which do not then go on to calculate how much it has cost. It will be quicker and easier to deduce Cost of Quality figures from this information than to try to collect the information afresh.

For example, most businesses will record and report the number or level of customer complaints received in a given period, often breaking these down into different categories of complaint. They may also measure how long, on average, it takes to deal with these complaints and what proportion are resolved to the apparent satisfaction of the customer. But it is much less common to see any assessment of the cost to the business of handling these complaints.

For the remaining activities, team members should use their interview results to arrive at estimates for each activity. It is important that they should not overlook their own time spent on any process activities, as well as that of their interviewees.

In all cases the costs must eventually be annualised. Figures from the payroll and other accounts department information should be taken from the most recent period available — preferably the last quarter — and then annualised. (It is essential to pay particular attention to any special seasonal considerations which may distort figures in any given period. Remember that a business with peak sales in December, for example, may experience peak supply problems four or five months earlier, with returns and warranty problems several months later. Checking back over previous full-year figures will reveal any significant trends). Figures derived from interviews, especially those relating to time costs, should also be multiplied out to develop an annual cost.

In some cases, the figures arrived at will be in the form of a literal cost, in other cases the figures will be shown in terms of quantities of materials or amounts of time.

The audit team must now use the information from the accounts department, as well as the salary bands and burden rates identified in Step 6, to convert these raw figures into monetary terms using a standard spreadsheet. Formulas will be crucial in helping to make future Cost of Quality assessments quicker and easier to conduct. For example, at the next assessment, interviewees need only be asked how much time they now spend on each of the activities they had previously identified. Similarly, the cost of materials in stock can easily be re-calculated in future by noting the new amounts. (Eventually, inflation-linked adjustments will need to be built-in here).

Note that the interviews did not touch on the intangible or "opportunity" costs explained in Step 8. The audit team will have to make an allowance for these costs. Since this is the most difficult area to define, and because of the potential for double-counting, it may be appropriate for the supervisory team to call together all the audit teams to agree a common standard for arriving at intangible costs. This standard will vary widely from business to business and from sector to sector. (For example, a supplier of machine parts to four large industrial customers will treat the loss of one of those customers very differently from a hotel group that loses the future custom of one guest). See also the note on "opportunity" costs in Step 8 above.

Figure 11 shows a time allocation schedule for a specific manufacturing process. The spreadsheet converts the time spent by different groups of staff into an actual salary expense. The spreadsheet includes separate headings for each of the four Cost of Quality categories — Prevention, Appraisal, Internal Failure and External Failure. Separate spreadsheets should be created to cover out-of-pocket expenses and other intangible expenses.

Step 10 Summary: *The audit team uses the data derived from interviews, combined with figures from the accounts department and management information reports, to calculate financial equivalents for each of the costs identified in the assessment.*

ALLOCATION SCHEDULE AND COMPUTATION OF COST OF QUALITY

	PERCENTAGE OF TIME SPENT ON DIFFERENT TYPES OF WORK						SALARY EXPENSE RELATED TO COST OF QUALITY						
Category	Number of Employees	Normal Work	Prevention	Appraisal	Internal Failure	External Failure	Prevention	Appraisal	Internal Failure	External Failure	Total Cost of Quality	Total Salary	CoQ/Salary
Confidential	3	100					0	0	0	0	0		
	3						0	0	0	0	0	252,034	0.00%
Exempt													
South Maintenance - 6040	6	30	55		15		125,268	0	34,164	0	159,432		
North Maintenance - 6050	6	63	30		7		68,328	0	15,943	0	84,271		
Construction Shop - 6011	3	80			20		0	0	22,76	0	22,776		
Machine Shop- 6012	3	40		40	20		0	45,552	22,776	0	68,320		
AC, Plumbing Heating - 6526	1	60			40		0	0	15,184	0	15,184		
Plant Engineering	1	0	60	30	10		22,776	11,388	3,796	0	37,960	759,200	
	20						216,372	56,940	114,639	0	387,951		51.10%
Non-Exempt							0	0					
Personal Assistant	1	100					0	0	0	0	0	25,875	
	1								0	0	0		0.00%
Hourly													
South Maintenance - 6040	41	30	55		15		712,941	0	194,438	0	907,379		
North Maintenance - 6050	58	63	30		7		550,118	0	128,341	0	678,479		
Central Maintenance - 6050	7	30	55		15		121,722	0	33,197	0	154,919		
MM Maintenance - 6070	26	30	55		15		139,110	0	37,939	0	177,049		
IN Maintenance - 6090	26	30	55		15		452,109	0	123,302	0	575,411		
Carpenter Shop - 6003	2	80			20		0	0	12,646	0	12,646		
Construction Shop 6011													
Environmental Maintenance	12	95			5		0	0	18,970	0	18,970		
Fabricators	4	95			5		0	0	9,485	0	9,485		
Concrete Crew	4	75			25		0	0	31,616	0	31,616		
Duct Work	5	85	5	10			7,904	15,808	0	0	23,712		
Roofing	4	100					0	0	0	0	0		
Construction	20	50			50		0	0	316,160	0	316,160		
Cleanup	4	100					0	0	0	0	0		
Machine Shop- 6012	33	40		40	20		0	417,331	208,666	0	625,997		
Mold Boring Shop-6013	9	90		10			0	28,454	0	0	28,454		
Machine Tool & Repairs - 6014	13	100					0	0	0	0	0		
AC, Plumbing, Heating - 6526	7	60			40		0	0	88,325	0	88,525		
Building Maintenance - 6530	5	20			80		0	0	126,464	0	126,464		
Plant Engineering - 6555	1	0	100				31,616	0	0	0	31,616		
	265						2,015,520	461,593	1,329,769	0	3,806,882	8,378,240	45.44%
	289						2,231,892	518,533	1,444,408	0	4,194,033	9,415,349	44.55%
							53.2%	12.4%	34.4%	0.0%			

Figure 11: Allocation Schedule and Computation of Cost of Quality

Step 11

PREPARING THE AUDIT REPORT

Once all interviews are complete, and all additional information has been collected, the audit team should begin to prepare its report. The intention here is to analyse the data obtained and present a clear summary of results, with detailed back-up documentation. This may be required by the supervisory team in order to reconcile the different costs and estimates presented by each audit team.

The main part of the report should describe and illustrate the process under assessment, paying attention to any areas where the process was truncated as discussed in Step 6. It should then go straight on to an assessment of costs, presented as they have been calculated. Clearly identify the process under examination and account for costs by the four categories of Prevention, Appraisal, Internal and External failure.

- Show the percentage and currency value of tangible, out-of-pocket expenses (materials/ supplies/services) allocated to each of the four Quality categories in a pie chart.
- Show the percentage of staff time allocated to Quality costs and its currency value (including the calculated burden rate) for each Quality category in a pie chart.
- Show the currency value of intangible "opportunity" costs.

Combine all these costs to present a total Cost of Quality for the process, broken down into the four Quality categories, again using a pie chart.

Then describe the key sources of substantial costs, noting any particular process components identified by the audit team as contributing substantially to Quality costs.

Finally note any reservations or qualifications that may apply to the figures and make any recommendations for future assessments or for action based on the assessment results with which the whole team agrees.

Reserve a detailed breakdown of all Quality costs, including spreadsheet information like that shown in Figure 11, the results of the individual interviews, and comments relating to any assumptions made during the course of their preparation and allocation, for an appendix to the assessment report. A note of any problems or concerns encountered during the course of the assessment should also be placed in the appendix. It may also be appropriate in the case of high-cost areas to outline any obvious obstacles to immediate improvement.

Finally, when submitting the report, the audit team should be sure to retain copies of all working papers and documents which may be needed to justify the figures reported or for future assessments.

Step 11 Summary: *The audit team prepares a concise report with all the relevant Quality-related costs and highlighting potential improvement targets.*

Step 12

PREPARING THE COMBINED AUDIT REPORT

On receipt of all the audit reports, each member of the supervisory team should be given time to read the reports. After an initial meeting, the supervisory team should decide whether to call in audit team representatives for further clarification of any of the figures and conclusions that have been presented. Unusual or unexpected items should be carefully noted.

For example, if appraisal costs are found to exceed failure costs, particular care should be taken to re-examine the costings. Either significant failure costs will have been overlooked or wrongly-classified, or the company should immediately consider how to transfer some of the resources currently allocated to appraisal to a more effective role in preventing faults, errors or failure.

Before starting to draft the final report, the supervisory team should refer again to the mission statement developed in Step 3 of the audit. They should also consider closely how they are going to present conclusions to the company.

Reducing the Cost of Quality must be the organisation's main priority on completion of the audit. But this is not to say that it must be treated as a cost reduction exercise. Instructing people ("stop doing this" or "don't allow that") may deliver some short-term cost reductions, but it will make substantial, long-term improvements much harder.

Allocating Responsibility for Improvement

It will be salutary for the supervisory team and for all senior management to accept responsibility themselves for the costs that have been uncovered. From this perspective, reducing the Cost of Quality needs to be viewed as a self-improvement exercise. "What can we do to improve the way we manage processes to prevent that happening?" "How can we invest in our staff so they are better equipped to find solutions?" The costs of training and restructuring are all, of course, prevention costs. But investing in prevention is the only way to drive down failure and rework costs effectively.

Part of this process must be the empowerment of staff. The initial Cost of Quality assessments will have gone some way towards creating a sense of empowerment. The people involved, who may have been complaining about errors and inefficiencies for years, should at last begin to feel that they can have some real influence in changing things. It is they who mapped the process, they who measured and calculated the Cost of Quality. Now it is they who must find and implement ways to improve performance and cut waste. If management's response is to impose change, management will then have to monitor these changes to make sure they happen and continue to happen. This will be an inspection cost. If staff suggest and adopt change, it is more likely to work and will not increase inspection costs.

The lesson to be learned is that the final Cost of Quality audit report must not be too prescriptive. Certainly it should draw conclusions from the audit. Certainly it should recommend areas where changes must be made fast. But it should not assume responsibility for deciding what those changes must be in detail. Otherwise it risks imposing yet another cumbersome and unworkable framework on top of others that may already exist.

Instead, responsibility must be handed back to the audit teams and to staff working on each business process. "You identified these problems. Now please identify some solutions. If these solutions require money or investment, we'll provide it (up to a certain maximum). It's up to you to make your chosen solutions work."

Opportunities for Improvement

There are many opportunities for investment in prevention, all of which should deliver consequential savings in failure costs. They include:

- paying more to hire or retain qualified and experienced staff
- encouraging and sharing the cost of continuing education for employees
- increasing the level of targeted internal training
- developing coordinated Quality improvement initiatives with key suppliers.

The Contents of the Combined Audit Report

The combined audit report itself, like the individual audit reports, should therefore contain two main elements:

- A concise summary of the relevant Cost of Quality statistics, presented graphically in a way that is clear to all members of staff. Pie charts will be helpful. A histogram showing the relationship of prevention, appraisal and failure costs and indicating the team's intentions for the future may be useful. Finally, present the Cost of Quality as a proportion of turnover or some other key indicator. The supervisory team may consider calculating it against labour costs, net sales, profit, etc. Whatever indicator is chosen, it is important to note that the figure is, at this stage incomplete. The audit has not measured the whole Cost of Quality for the company, merely the costs associated with those business processes identified for assessment.

- A statement of intent, as discussed earlier in Step 12, which accepts responsibility for the costs identified, outlines improvement opportunities, states the management's willingness to fund investment in cost reduction, and hands back responsibility for delivering improvement to the staff involved.

As with the individual audit reports, detailed Cost of Quality figures and spreadsheet information should be reserved for an appendix.

Before presenting the report to the company as a whole, it will be important to add the CEO's signature to the document, or to its preface, clearly demonstrating commitment at the most senior levels of the company to making sure that the results of the audit are not wasted.

Step 12 Summary: *The supervisory team should prepare a short clear report which clearly shows the costs that have been uncovered, and looks towards the next stage in the improvement process.*

Step 13

SHARING THE FINDINGS AND TAKING ACTION

The report should now be presented first to the CEO and senior management team, then to the company as a whole (either by the supervisory team or by the managers who briefed the company at Step 5).

The presentation to the CEO and senior management team can, and should, lead to serious questioning of the report's assumptions and to a reappraisal of the company's overall business strategy and performance. The supervisory team should be prepared to answer questions about the possibility of integrating the Cost of Quality measures into a Total Quality, Re-engineering or other company-wide improvement programme.

The presentation to staff should be done as soon as possible, as the interviews will have generated considerable interest among staff and the supervisory team needs to capitalise on that enthusiasm in moving forward to seek cost improvements. The presentation should follow the same approach as the report itself, highlighting key costs and focusing on the role of staff in identifying and implementing process improvements.

Management and staff must be reminded that the costs identified in the audit are not definitive, that a number of significant costs may have been overlooked, and that the audit only relates to certain core processes. Staff should be encouraged to identify and report new factors contributing to the Cost of Quality in their area and, most importantly, to suggest ways in which those costs could be addressed. (For this reason, it will often be found that the second and even third Cost of Quality audits suggest a higher overall Cost of Quality as new costs are identified. It is, therefore, important to prepare people for this prospect to avoid disillusion or disappointment.)

Just as the audit report must not prescribe solutions, so the presentation must also be careful not to do so. At the presentation, it should be announced that the audit teams will now be asked to develop specific recommendations for improving the process on which they were working, and they will develop these recommendations in conjunction with the process staff that they interviewed during the assessments. No more than a month should be allowed for these recommendations to be presented.

After receiving top-level approval for any expenditure that may be required to implement these recommendations, a full Cost of Quality improvement initiative will have begun.

Note that many staff recommendations in the early stages of the Cost of Quality initiative may focus attention on the cost savings to be derived from a "Just-in-Time" approach. Equally, in a manufacturing company, the importance will be seen of streamlining research, design and manufacture using any of the techniques of Simultaneous or Concurrent Engineering. The supervisory team should look for common themes to be found in the improvement suggestions that are made, so that the whole company can begin to benefit from the best ideas that are being applied to specific processes. In all cases, it will be essential for the supervisory team to credit fully the staff who initially developed these "bandwagon" suggestions.

Step 13 Summary: *The audit report is presented as soon as possible to senior management and then to the whole company, emphasising the crucial importance of the coming round of cost improvements.*

Step 14

Developing a Continuing Cycle of Audit and Improvement

The Cost of Quality improvement initiative started in Step 13 should immediately begin to drive future audits, as the supervisory team and individual process teams seek confirmation that the changes being made are delivering real improvements and cost savings.

This initiative will obviously be considerably helped by the support and commitment of top management, but the principal driver should always be the process staff themselves. To this end, the supervisory team may find it useful to display Cost of Quality measures and improvement targets and results publicly and prominently. As well as making results available via the intranet, consider using large poster size charts to communicate basic data to anyone who has not been directly involved in the Cost of Quality assessment.

The audit cycle will vary from company to company and on the time available, as well as on the speed with which changes can be expected to happen. It is important to avoid measuring costs that cannot be expected to have changed, but frustrating not to measure ones that have changed. As a general rule, individual processes should be assessed at least every six months, or more frequently if there is any expectation of faster results. Overall, it may not be necessary to produce a full audit report for all processes more often than once a year.

As results begin to be seen, management and staff should both want to see the assessments extended to new business processes not covered in the first audit.

Refining Cost of Quality Measures

During each business process assessment, it may have been noticed that particular tasks or activities have a high level of Quality costs associated with them. In the model presented here, no effort has been made to break down Quality costs by activity — simply to apportion an overall Cost of Quality to a core business process.

But once a regular audit cycle has been established, it may be useful to focus on those high-cost areas using Activity Based Costing (ABC). ABC uses exactly the same measures as a regular Cost of Quality audit to achieve a different result.

Process costing (the approach used in this self-assessment guide) tends to focus attention on efficiency — how well a particular process is performed. What it does not do is to focus attention on the usefulness of that process or of particular tasks or activities within the process. For example, process costing will help to reduce the overall Cost of Quality associated with supplying a complex, one-off product or service. ABC will enable management to find out whether the associated Cost of Quality actually makes it uneconomic to supply that product/service.

ABC is much closer to traditional cost accounting measures than process costing and it may, at first sight, seem more attractive to management. However, experience suggests that it is preferable first to reduce the overall Cost of Quality as far as possible before making judgements about the cost-effectiveness or viability of a particular task. For this reason, process costing should always be introduced and established first.

Step 14 Summary: *Given the right commitment and support from the top, results from the first Cost of Quality audit should provide the motivation for an ongoing round of assessment and improvement.*

Avoiding the Pitfalls of a Cost of Quality Audit

Two potential problems have already been referred to: the danger of top management misunderstanding the purpose of the audit, and the objections that staff may raise. Senior management should also be aware of the following potential problems:

1. Be careful when using Cost of Quality data as a benchmarking comparison.

Cost of Quality is most commonly expressed as a percentage of company turnover (see the figures cited at the start of this self-assessment guide). But companies operating in different sectors must expect different levels of Cost of Quality. A manufacturer of sophisticated military equipment should expect to find a higher Cost of Quality than a producer of kitchen towels. Similarly, companies operating in the same sector but providing different "grades" of service will find differing levels of Cost. Even considering the higher rates charged, a 5-Star hotel will have to face a proportionately higher Cost of Quality than a motel.

This raises several issues:

- Remember the need to focus on streamlining individual business processes.
- Be aware that internal comparisons between Quality costs associated with different processes can be damaging if carried out indiscriminately.
- The main use of a process cost measure must always be to develop strategies and tactics to drive down the Cost of Quality for that particular process — and then to measure the success that results from all of these improvement efforts. Benchmarking may then be used to copy the techniques themselves, rather than trying to match the levels of performance improvement dollar for dollar.
- It can be fruitless to try to identify a norm for each category of prevention, appraisal and failure costs. At the outset, it was suggested that a company's overall Cost of Quality was likely, on first assessment, to lie somewhere between 20% and 40% of turnover. This is intended only to reassure companies undertaking a Cost of Quality audit that such a figure is not surprising and to reassure those involved in the audit that they have not performed some alarming miscalculation.

2. Resist pressures to be too precise.

It has been shown that the audit must have the full support of finance/accounts staff. Even if this has been established at the outset, there is a danger that it will be lost when preparing the report on the overall Cost of Quality. So many assumptions and estimates will have been made, by different teams using different criteria, that the resulting figures will never have the accuracy required of a set of management accounts. For this reason, finance department staff may refuse to endorse the Cost of Quality figures.

Remember that there is no need to have precise figures. Indeed they could always be disputed. The object is to arrive at "ballpark" figures which give an indication of the scale of the problem. These will help in deciding whether the Cost of Quality is big enough to worry about (it will be), and which projects should be tackled as a matter of priority.

3. Always be consistent.

The most important element of a Cost of Quality audit cycle is consistency. It will not matter that the estimated Cost of Quality is 10% too high or too low. But it is essential that each subsequent assessment and audit uses the same measures and criteria so that measurement can be accurately and reliably calculated.

One reason why this self-assessment guide has stressed the process costing approach is the danger of becoming hypnotised by the resulting Cost of Quality estimate for the whole company. While it has been noted that uncovering an overall Cost of Quality of 25% or 30% of turnover can have substantial value, most benefit will be derived from observing and monitoring patterns, common elements and trends within the overall figure. Many of these patterns will be associated with individual process components or with groups of comparable processes.

4. Beware of using Cost of Quality data as a measure of individual effectiveness.

The audit will reveal data that can be used to help process team members to learn from each other.

Don't use assessment results from different processes competitively or to "punish" members of poorly-performing process teams. Cost of Quality is a company problem. If costs are concentrated in a particular department or process there will be a good reason for this which is almost never associated with the work or effectiveness of an individual or a group of people. If one person is found to be responsible for adding disproportionately to the Cost of Quality, managers should remember that this is their own responsibility. Does the individual have too much work?... or need more training?

Avoiding the competitive use of the Cost of Quality is one of the most important reasons why this self-assessment uses a process costing approach, rather than an activity-based or department-based approach. Process improvement involves people across departmental boundaries, so helping to improve teamwork and communication. These skills in themselves will help to reduce the Cost of Quality substantially.

5. Beware of misconceptions.

Auditing the Cost of Quality will not, in itself, solve anything. But it will help people at all levels of the company to see the significant impact on profitability of problems that were not previously classified as "Quality issues".

Summary

Measuring the Cost of Quality is a powerful tool in identifying areas for improvement:

- By converting problems that are often seen as endemic and inevitable into tangible costs, it enables senior management to see their real impact on profitability for the first time.
- By showing staff members that they can act on problems of waste, delay and inefficiency, it enables employees at all levels to take greater responsibility for the efficient running of the organisation.
- By focusing on business processes, it opens up a whole range of related improvement opportunities.
- By offering a continuing measure of improvement, it offers the means to build and maintain momentum in any Quality improvement programme.
- By focusing on the objective of 100% customer satisfaction, it virtually guarantees that customers will be happier with the product or service that they receive.

Many companies have audited their Cost of Quality and achieved dramatic improvements from the resulting Quality improvement initiative. Improvement statistics like this are in the grasp of any organisation that embarks on a continuing cycle of Cost of Quality audit and improvement.

Part 2

THE AUDIT PROCESS

This section addresses the logistical and process requirements of conducting an audit. The topics covered in this section include:

- Staffing the supervisory and audit teams
- Creating an audit project plan
- Laying the groundwork for the audit
- Analysing audit results
- Sharing audit results
- Writing effective audit reports
- Dealing with resistance to audit recommendations
- Building an ongoing audit programme

Staffing the Supervisory and Audit Teams

In addition to the advice in Part 1, Step 1 about the selection of a supervisory team to oversee the Cost of Quality audit and the selection of individual audit teams, this section contains some more general advice about the structure and make-up of both teams (remembering that, in smaller organisations, the supervisory team may conduct some or all of the audits itself).

The supervisory team will:

- Consist of three to four people.
- Report to the CEO or other senior executive.
- Represent a carefully selected range of skills and experience.

The audit team will be of a similar make-up, but will report to the supervisory team rather than to the CEO. More than four people may be needed for an audit team if data gathering is labour intensive, as when large numbers of customers or employees must be interviewed. However, audit teams of more than six or seven people present problems for maintaining uniformity and communicating audit progress and findings during the course of the evaluation.

Selecting an Audit Team Leader

The audit team leader will play an important role in shaping both the data gathering and the findings from the audit. The strength of the team leader will also influence the acceptance of the audit, both in terms of enlisting cooperation in the data gathering phase and in securing support for improvement initiatives that grow out of the audit. Because of the importance of this role, care should be taken in selecting the appropriate person for the job. Most successful audit team leaders:

- Have a good relationship with the executive-level sponsor of the audit.
- Are well-liked and well-respected at all levels of the organisation.
- Have good interpersonal skills and can maintain good relationships even in difficult circumstances.

- Have good analytical skills and can assimilate and process large amounts of complex data quickly.
- Have some knowledge of the function or area being audited.
- Have extensive knowledge of the type of process being audited.
- Communicate ideas clearly and effectively.

Skills to be Represented on the Supervisory Team and on the Audit Teams

Members of both supervisory and audit teams should be selected on the basis of what each can bring to the project. Selection efforts should focus on developing a balanced representation of the following qualities:

- A variety of tenures in the organisation, with relative newcomers preferably having experience in other organisations.
- A range of familiarity/experience with the area (function or site) being audited. Those who are intimately familiar with the area can serve as guides to the less familiar; those who are new to the area can provide objectivity and ask questions that might never be considered by those more involved in the area.
- Considerable familiarity with the type of process being audited. For this reason, many organisations call on people filling roles in similar processes from other parts of the company to work on audit teams.
- Good analytical skills.
- Good interpersonal skills.
- Good facilitation and interviewing skills.
- Good communication skills.
- An understanding of the company's strategy and direction.

Creating an Audit Project Plan

Creating an audit project plan accomplishes the following objectives:

- Ensures the allocation of adequate resources or helps supervisory and audit team members be prepared to improvise in the face of short resources.
- Ensures the audit is timed so resources are available that may be in high demand.
- Creates clear expectations in the minds of team members about what must be done, and when — especially important when they are not committed to the project full-time.
- Ensures accountability for what must be done, who is responsible for which tasks, and when the audit must be completed.

Financial audits often rely on the Critical Path Method (CPM) of project planning. This method was originally developed by the US Department of Defense to facilitate the timely completion of weapons development and production. It has since been modified to help in planning a wide variety of projects. The following outline is a simplification of CPM. It suggests the aspects of a project that should be taken into account during the planning phase.

Critical Path Method

In developing the project plan, audit team members should ask and answer the following questions:

- *What tasks must be performed?*

This list should include the major tasks outlined in the audits, along with sub-tasks that grow out of those major headings. It should also include any tasks mandated by unique circumstances in the company performing the self-assessment. The audit team may want to brainstorm about tasks that need to be performed, then refine the list to reflect the work priorities of the audit.

- *In what order will the tasks be completed?*

Answering this question should include an analysis of which tasks and sub-tasks are dependent on others. Which tasks cannot begin until another has been completed? Which tasks can be done at any time? The audit team may want to place the ordered task on a time line, with start dates, expected duration of the step and end dates outlined for each task.

- *Who will perform each task?*

Most tasks will be performed by members of the audit and assessment teams. These assignments should be based on the strengths of each team member as well as the amount of time they have available. Equity of work load should also be taken into account. If tasks are to be assigned to people not on the audit team, those individuals should be included or consulted at this point.

- *What resources will be needed for each step?*

Each task should be analysed in terms of the personnel, budget, equipment, facilities, support services and any other resources that will be needed for its completion. The team should assess the availability of all of the resources. Consideration should be given to the task ordering completed earlier. Are some resources subject to competing demands, and therefore difficult to secure at a particular time? How far in advance do arrangements for resources need to be made? Does the task order or time line need to be revised in light of what is known about resource availability?

- *Where is the slack time?*

Slack time is unscheduled time between dependent tasks. Slack provides a degree of flexibility in altering the start dates of subsequent tasks. Slack time signals that a task has a range of possible start dates. It is used to determine the critical path.

- *What is the critical path?*

The critical path in a project is the set of tasks that must be completed in a sequential, chronological order. If any task on the critical path is not completed, all subsequent tasks will be delayed. Delays at any point in the critical path will result in an equivalent delay in the completion of the total project.

Regardless of the method used to develop the project plan, no project, even the most simple, is ever completed in exact accordance with its plan. However, having a project plan allows the team to gauge its progress, anticipate problems and determine where alternative approaches are needed.

Laying the Groundwork for the Audit

Once the supervisory and audit teams have been selected and a project plan developed, the audit team leader should prepare those who will be involved in, and affected by, the audit for each team's visit or for data gathering. The following steps will help the audit to run more smoothly:

Communicate Executive Support for the Audit

Demonstrating executive support for the audit accomplishes two goals. First, it increases the chances that those involved in the area being audited will cooperate with data-gathering efforts. Second, it shows executive support for the area being audited and suggests a commitment to improving performance in that area.

In many companies, the audit programme is introduced by the executive sponsor of the audit by means of an intranet webcast or a more conventional written or multimedia presentation. The presentation should explain the purpose of the audit and ask for the support of everyone in the area being audited. It should be seen by everyone within the company who will be affected by, or involved in, the data gathering process. The most effective presentations explain how the audit results will be used, reassuring those who will be responding to audit team requests about the motives of the audit. Credibility is also bolstered when previous audits have been acted upon with positive results.

Make Arrangements with the Area to Be Audited

The audit team leader should check with the appropriate manager in charge of the process or site being audited to arrange for any required on-site visits, interviewing, surveys, focus groups or written information needed for the audit. The team leader should also explain the purpose, scope and expected duration of the audit; review the project plan with the manager; and answer any questions the manager has about the audit.

The team leader should also work with the appropriate manager or managers to determine how the audit can be conducted with the least impact on the flow of work. This may include discussions about the timing of the audit, the options for data gathering, the availability of needed data and possibilities for generating the necessary information quickly and easily. Finding ways to make data collection more efficient and effective is especially important when the audit is part of an ongoing programme, rather than an isolated assessment.

Develop a Protocol or Checklist

A protocol or checklist can be used by the audit team to outline the issues that are central to the audit. Written guides can help the leaders of those areas being audited to prepare for the audit. A protocol represents a plan of what the audit team will do to accomplish the objectives of the audit. It is an important tool of the audit, since it not only serves as the audit team's guide to collecting data, but also as a record of the audit procedures completed by the team. In many cases, audit teams may want to format the checklist in a way that allows them to enter their field notes directly on an electronic checklist.

The checklist should include no more than twenty major items, and checklists should be updated with each audit in order to ensure that the appropriate measures are taken. Items where improvement initiatives have been successful should be eliminated from the checklist, with newly identified possibilities for improvement opportunities added.

Analysing Audit Results

Discovering gaps between a company's targets and its actual performance is a relatively easy task. Tools are provided to assist audit teams in assessing their performance in a given area. In most cases, more opportunities for improvement will be uncovered by an audit than can be addressed by the resources and energy available. Therefore, one of the most difficult aspects of analysing the results of an audit lies in determining which opportunities are the most important for managers to pursue.

Because resources and energy for pursuing improvement initiatives are limited, choices must be made about which options are most important. Sometimes these decisions are based on political winds in the company, or on what has worked well in the past, or on personal preferences of top management. However, scarce resources will be used more effectively if allocated to the areas where they will have the greatest impact. Managers must also determine the most effective way to approach initiatives. This section discusses criteria for prioritising opportunities that grow out of audit findings.

The Novations Strategic Alignment Model

For many years the "excellence" movement encouraged companies to achieve excellence in every area of endeavour. Although the movement created an awareness of the need for management improvements, it failed to recognise that management processes are not all equal in terms of producing benefits. As a result, leading organisations today focus on performing well in a few core areas. Knowing what those core areas are depends on a clear vision of the company's strategy.

Strategic thinking about which areas should be improved involves much more than taking an inventory of current capabilities and weaknesses. If it did not, existing capabilities would always determine strategic objectives, and organisational growth and development would come to a halt. In setting priorities strategically, we use the Novations Group's Strategic Alignment Model. According to this model, companies must allocate improvement opportunities to one of the following categories:

- Those they should do themselves.
- Those they should do with someone else.

- Those they should contract others to do.
- Those they should not do.

At the same time, all work can be allocated to one of four categories:

Unit of Competitive Advantage (UCA) Work includes work and capabilities that create distinctiveness for the business in the marketplace.

Value-Added Support Work facilitates the accomplishment of UCA work. For example, a company may have a technology orientation rather than a service orientation, but an effective logistics process may help them to improve their UCA work of providing cutting-edge technology.

Essential Support Work neither creates advantage nor facilitates the work that creates advantage, but must be done if businesses are to continue to operate (includes such things as paying taxes, maintaining payroll records, etc.).

Non-Essential Work is activity that has lost its usefulness but continues to be done out of habit or tradition.

Despite their sophistication in dealing with other aspects of business, most managers have archaic views of the different types of work. Many of their models for characterising work have come from a finance or accounting orientation. Accounting terms such as overhead, direct labour and indirect labour may be useful as a way to report costs, but they provide little understanding about the relative strategic importance of the work. Yet these classifications are frequently used to determine how work is organised and where resources are allocated.

The concept of unit of competitive advantage (UCA) helps to explain why some organisations either emphasise the wrong capabilities or de-emphasise the right capabilities. UCA also explains why some forms of improvement lead to competitive disadvantage, and why some businesses consistently outperform their competitors by gaining greater leverage from their competitive advantages.

A company's UCA includes the critical processes that create distinctiveness within an established strategic direction. It is based on the premise that businesses create competitive advantage when they focus their attention on a few key processes and implement those key processes in world-class fashion. For example, continuous improvement is a popular management programme that assumes benefit from any kind of ongoing improvement. Generally speaking, however, continuous improvement programmes will only create competitive advantage when an organisation defines a strategic direction, clarifies strategic objectives, and determines its UCA. These crucial prerequisites tell where continuous improvement efforts should be focused to create maximum leverage. They suggest what kinds of work to improve interdependently, what kinds to improve separately, and what kinds not to waste time on. They even signal when continuous improvement is more likely to create competitive disadvantage rather than competitive advantage.

UCA Initiatives Should Take Priority

Understanding what work falls into which categories requires a clear understanding of the company's strategy. The initiatives resulting from an audit that affect the Unit of Competitive Advantage work processes should clearly have the highest priority among improvement projects. Value-added support initiatives should be second priority, and essential support work should be the third priority. Non-essential work should not be continued.

Once improvement opportunities that will have the greatest impact on the achievement of the company's goals have been identified, the following ideas can be used to lend further insight into how opportunities identified through an audit should be prioritised:

- *Focus on the two or three most important areas.*

Insisting that action be taken on all of the problems uncovered by the audit may overwhelm the people who are responsible for bringing about those changes. Flatter organisations and leaner work forces mean that people are already being asked to do more work with fewer resources and less time. Producing a long list of improvement initiatives may prompt people to dismiss all of them because they don't have time to complete the whole list.

- *Focus on the areas that can be changed.*

Emphasising problems that are beyond the control of the people who are responsible for working on process improvement only leads to cynicism and a sense of powerlessness. By focusing on things that are within the sphere of influence, accountability for each part of the action plan can be clearly defined.

- *Include as priorities some improvements that can be made quickly.*

Rapid, visible improvement helps build support for more complicated initiatives. Quick improvements also reassure people of management's support for long-term improvement. Seeing immediate improvement helps to build commitment to the process at all levels and helps build momentum for further change.

- *Emphasise the improvements that seem essential to long-term success.*

Essential improvements may involve sensitive issues or difficult problems, such as deficiencies in fundamental skill levels within the organisation or basic strategy issues. These problems are not only difficult and expensive to address, but may also cause a great deal of personal pain or require significant individual adjustment. Nevertheless, long-term improvement requires a commitment to dealing with difficult issues rather than avoiding them.

Sharing Audit Results

In most cases, audit results will be presented to various interested people in a feedback meeting before they are made fully available online. As a rule, the overall results for the organisation will be reported and presented first, while audit results will be discussed with individual process groups afterwards.

When reporting overall results, those in attendance may include members of the executive team, managers who work in the area covered by the audit, the audit and supervisory team members, and anyone else who is affected by or interested in the results. The meeting should be conducted by members of the supervisory audit team. The purpose is to present their findings, and make recommendations for capitalising on opportunities for improvement.

Conducting Effective Feedback Meetings

The strategy for the meeting should be to present a clear and simple picture of the current situation as revealed by the audit. This may be a moment of truth for those who have been anticipating the audit results. The feedback meeting for an audit holds both excitement and anxiety: excitement that the future will be bright, and anxiety that shortcomings in individual performance will be highlighted and demands made for personal change. As a result, the meeting must be carefully managed in order to lead to productive change. The following structure is one recommended format for conducting a feedback meeting.

- *Introduce the meeting and preview its agenda.*

This might include an overview of the original intent of the audit, introduction of the audit team, and a brief summary of the meeting's agenda. This step should take no more than five minutes.

- *Present the audit findings.*

Audit findings should summarise the most important points revealed by the data gathered in the audit process. They should be presented separately from the audit recommendations in order to allow people to digest the two parts of the presentation separately. Clearing up misunderstandings about the findings may make the group more accepting of the team's recommendations.

The presentation of the audit findings should take comparatively little time. Audits almost always generate much more data than can be effectively presented or digested in a feedback meeting. The goal of the audit team should be to home in on the two or three most important points learned from the audit, and present enough supporting data to illustrate those points.

Presenting too much data about audit findings has a number of negative effects. It encourages people to conduct their own analysis of the audit data. To a certain extent, this is a healthy and normal reaction. If others understand the evidence that supports the conclusions drawn by the audit team, they are more likely to accept and "own" the audit results. Therefore, they will be more committed to the changes brought about by the audit results. However, when people immerse themselves in large amounts of data, they may become victims of "analysis paralysis": they may spend unnecessary time attempting to explain contradictory data, or trying to understand methods used by others to gather data.

- *Present audit recommendations.*

Presenting the audit recommendations should be the central point of the meeting. The recommendations should grow out of the data highlights presented. The supervisory team should view the recommendations as discussion points for the meeting rather than as absolute action items.

A common mistake in feedback meetings is to spend most of the meeting on presenting data and recommendations. It is easy for audit and supervisory team members to become enamoured of data they have invested considerable time and energy in collecting and analysing. Others in the audience will probably also be interested in the details of the data collected. However, if too much time is spent on discussing the recommendations, the meeting will end before a commitment to action has been made.

- *Ask others to react to the data.*

The reactions of top management and those responsible for implementing audit recommendations will determine the ultimate value of the audit data. So the feedback meeting is a good time to resolve questions or problems about the findings and recommendations as they have been presented. If resistance to the audit findings is not resolved in the feedback meeting, opportunities for improvement may be lost.

Those attending the meeting may offer their opinions willingly. If not, the audit team members should ask the others in the room for their reaction to what has been presented.

- *Develop preliminary action plans.*

The detailed action plans should grow out of the recommendations made by the audit team. They should specifically address the question of who should do what by when. Formal accountability mechanisms should be established before the end of the meeting, such as the scheduling of subsequent meetings or follow-up check points.

Sharing reports more widely

The same rules that apply to the critical feedback meeting apply to the sharing of audit results across the organisation.

While it is important to make the key data, principal conclusions and preliminary action plans quickly available online, it is distracting and unhelpful to provide or circulate too much data. Once again, staff are likely to be distracted by the possibility of over-analysing the data or engaging in protracted discussion of alternative interpretations when they don't fully understand the nature of the process being audited.

Of course, it is also important that staff working in the areas and processes that have been audited should not feel blamed for systematic problems or weaknesses. On the contrary, the most effective presentation of audit results will clearly highlight improvements that can result from the audit and generate enthusiasm for the audit process in other areas of the organisation. The next section contains further information on this topic.

Preparing Effective Audit Reports

There are three fundamental reasons for preparing a formal report at the end of an audit and these apply to individual audit reports as well as to the supervisory team's overall report:

- An audit report may be a stand-alone summary of the audit. This approach is not recommended, inasmuch as the report is likely to be filed away, making further action unlikely.
- The report may supplement a feedback meeting, providing those in attendance with documentation and an outline to follow.
- The report should also serve as a baseline document to make measurement of performance improvement possible in future audits.

Because the written report is the most enduring part of the audit presentation, it should be well written and easy to understand. The following tips will help in the preparation of effective written audit reports.

Focus on a Few Key Points

The audit presentation should focus on the two or three most important findings. It is impossible to present all of the data gathered in the audit to those who were not on the audit team. It is also not advisable to present every detail of the data. The audit team members should trust their own judgment about what the highlights of the study were, and present enough data to support that judgment. For each of the major findings, the team may want to include the following information:

- What is the problem?
- Why does it exist?
- What happens if the problem is not fixed:
  - in the short term?
  - in the long term?
- Recommend solutions.
- Outline expected benefits.

Prepare an Outline Before Preparing the First Draft

A good outline ensures that the logic of the report is clear, and that ideas proceed in an order that makes sense. The following outline provides one approach that works effectively.

Background

This section should establish the framework for the audit in terms of:

- Providing a brief discussion of the overall purpose of the audit.
- Identifying the role of the audit team in the overall process.
- Establishing the limitations of the audit methodology to ensure that others use the results provided in the report appropriately.

Objectives

This section should identify specific objectives of the audit in terms of types of information the team was expected to generate.

Methodology

The methodology section should describe the mechanics of the audit and include the following information:

- Types of assessment used (survey, interviews, focus groups, etc.).
- Data sources, or the sample groups for each of the types of assessment used.
- Time frame during which the audit was conducted.
- Other pertinent details about how the audit was conducted.

Findings

This section is designed to provide others with a review of the "facts" that came out of the audit. Except in cases where an audit checks regulatory compliance, only the most significant findings should be discussed in any detail in the report. This section should also include briefly presented data supporting the findings.

Conclusions

This section should report the audit team's interpretation of what the facts of the audit mean in light of the objectives stated at the outset of the audit.

Recommendations

This section includes suggestions from the supervisory or audit team on how to close the performance gaps identified in the audit. The degree of detail to be included in the audit report will vary from company to company and audit to audit.

Appendix

This portion of the formal report should include any of the following items that are relevant to the audit:

- A copy of any questionnaires or survey instruments used in the audit.
- A summary of the data gathered in the course of the audit.
- Recommendations for subsequent audits based on the team's experience.

Present Audit Findings Accurately

Those who read the report will no doubt be somewhat familiar with the area covered by the audit. They may notice discrepancies between what they know about the subject and what is reported in the written document. Spotting one inaccuracy may lead the readers to discredit all of the findings, conclusions and recommendations. Audit team members should be careful to report data as it was actually generated, and to describe the impact of the findings accurately.

Use Clear, Concise Language

Every statement included in the report should be based on sound evidence developed or reviewed during the audit. Whatever is said must be supported or supportable. Speculation should be avoided. Generalities and vague reporting will only confuse and mislead those that the report should influence or inform. For example, a report using the terms some, a few, or not all can leave the reader confused about the significance of the finding. Specific quantities should be used, such as, "of the ten samples taken, two were found to be...", "Three of five respondents said that...", and so on. Statements should be qualified as needed, and any unconfirmed data or information should be identified as such.

Ideas that do not amplify the central theme should be eliminated. The report should not identify individuals or highlight the mistakes of individuals.

Use Good Grammar and Style

Basic rules should be followed in preparing the report. Below are some examples:

- Avoid extreme terms, such as alarming, deplorable, gross negligence, etc.
- Avoid using redundant or lengthy phrases, such as calling something an emergency situation when the word emergency alone will do.
- Avoid verbs camouflaged as nouns or adjectives. For example, use "the

new procedure will reduce errors," rather than "The new procedure will accomplish a reduction of error entries."

- Use short, familiar words. Use words that are easily understandable to everyone and that convey the message concisely. Just because it is a formal report, do not write 'persons', 'beverages' or 'engage in a dialogue' when you mean 'people', 'drinks' and 'talk'.
- Keep sentences short. Most writing experts suggest that an average sentence should be no more than 15 to 18 words long. Packing too many ideas into a single sentence confuses and tires readers.

The audit team should provide enough background information in the report so that the reader clearly understands who conducted the audit and what the audit did or did not include. The purpose of the report as well as the purpose and scope of the audit should also be described in a manner that tells the reader why the report was written and who should take corrective action.

Timing of the Report

The timing of audit reports is critical to the overall reporting process and must be carefully thought out. In many cases, a written draft of the audit report is prepared one to three weeks before the feedback meeting. This draft then goes through a review and another report is prepared in time for the team's presentation. A final report may be completed after the feedback session has been held in order to record changes resulting from that meeting.

Presentation of the Report

The audit report will probably be made available on the company intranet to all interested employees, often with a short summary linking to more detailed conclusions and relevant audit data.

However, just as the audit programme will normally have been introduced by means of a webcast or similar online presentation, so it will be useful for the same individual to make a brief presentation of the audit's conclusions. This will provide a measure of continuity and ensure that the audit team has the chance to emphasise the benefits of the audit to the business as a whole and to reassure those staff who may have lingering concerns that the audit is a veiled attempt to justify cut-backs or job-losses. A live question and answer session will also be useful if team members sense significant levels of concern or resistance amongst staff (see the next section)

Presented thoughtfully, the audit results can help to underline the company's commitment to its strategic objectives and help to generate increased commitment and participation at all levels of the organisation.

Dealing with Resistance to Recommendations

Most audit teams feel that if they can present their ideas clearly and logically, and have the best interests of the company or department at heart, managers will accept the recommendations made as part of the audit and follow the team's recommendations. Many people who have worked in organisations, however, find that no matter how reasonably recommendations are presented, they are all too often not implemented.

Implementation usually fails because it requires people to change their ways of working. That change requires a great deal of effort, energy and risk; therefore, change is usually resisted. Resistance is an emotional process; people may embrace recommendations based on their logic, but fail to implement them because of emotional resistance to the personal change involved. Resistance is a predictable, natural and necessary part of the learning process. Although resistance may cause audit team members to feel they have missed the mark in terms of the recommendations they have made, it actually often signals accuracy in having interpreted the organisation's needs. By dealing with the resistance directly, audit teams can work through barriers to implementing process improvements.

What Are the Signs of Resistance?

In many cases, resistance may be expressed directly. Direct objections to recommendations are relatively easy to address as they can be discussed and resolved. When recommendations are being presented in the initial meeting, team members should stop frequently to allow those who are listening to the report to voice any objections or disagreements. Those who are presenting the data should be careful not to become defensive or to criticise those who express reservations about the recommendations. It is impossible to deal with objections unless they are voiced; so the audit or supervisory team should welcome the expression of objections or differences of opinion. The following tips may be used to uncover and deal with direct resistance:

- Provide many opportunities for others to express their concerns.
- Carefully clarify any confusing concerns.
- Deal with important or easy concerns immediately. Defer the remainder.

- Summarise the concerns before moving on. Show that concerns have been heard.

If direct resistance continues, the following steps may be necessary:

- Talk about the differences of opinion.
- Voice concern and support for negotiating a resolution.
- Avoid struggles for control of the situation.

Dealing with Indirect Resistance

In other cases, resistance may be subtle and elusive. Indirect resistance is difficult to identify and deal with. People who are experiencing indirect resistance may feel that they are "getting the run around". Many different forms of resistance may manifest themselves at the first meeting or more widely across the company:

- Requests for more detail.
- Providing too much detail in response to questions.
- Complaining that there isn't enough time to implement recommendations.
- Claiming that the recommendations are impractical.
- Attacking those who propose improvement initiatives.
- Acting confused.
- Responding with silence.
- Intellectualising about the data.
- Moralising that problems wouldn't exist if it weren't for "those people".
- Agreeing to implement recommendations with no intention of acting on them.
- Asking questions about methodology.
- Arguing that previous problems have resolved themselves.
- Focusing on solutions before findings are fully understood.

Almost any of these responses is legitimate in moderate amounts. For example, members of the group may have concerns about the audit's methodology that should be considered. Managers may realistically wonder where they will find the time to implement recommendations. However, if refusal to act on recommendations persists once legitimate concerns have been addressed, then the audit team is probably facing indirect resistance.

Many models used in sales training provide recommendations for overcoming resistance. These methods suggest the use of data and logical arguments to win the point and convince the other person to buy whatever is being sold. These models work well for direct resistance. However, indirect resistance is normally based on feelings rather than logic. So the only way to truly overcome resistance is to deal with the emotional processes that caused it in the first place. It is almost impossible to talk people out of the way they feel.

Feelings pass and change when they are expressed directly. A key skill for audit teams attempting to implement recommendations is to ask the people who are presenting resistance to put directly into words what they are experiencing. The following keys provide help in uncovering and dealing with indirect resistance.

- *Work once or twice with the person's concern, even when it feels as if he or she is resisting recommendations.*

By attempting to work with the problem stated by the person raising a concern, audit team members can determine whether the concern is legitimate or whether it is an excuse for not taking action. If the issues raised are legitimate, the person should show some willingness to discuss and resolve them. If the issues are manifestations of indirect resistance, the person will probably respond with other forms of resistance.

- *Identify the form the resistance is taking.*

Paying attention to the dynamics of a discussion can provide important clues as to whether or not someone is resisting recommendations. If they consistently distance themselves from those who are presenting the audit findings, using gestures or postures that suggest tension or discomfort, while at the same time presenting arguments for why the recommendations presented are inappropriate, it is probably a sign of resistance. The non-verbal responses of the presenters may also signal the onset of resistance. If presenters feel that they are suppressing negative feelings or becoming bored or irritated, it may be further evidence that those listening are resisting.

Once presenters become aware of the resistance, the next step is to put it into words. This is best done by using neutral, everyday language. The skill is to describe the form of the resistance in a way that encourages the other person to make a more direct statement of the reservation he or she is experiencing.

A useful guideline is to restate the resistant statement in common, non-threatening language. Statements should be made in the same tone and language that would be used to address a problem with a close friend. The statement should be made with as little evaluation as possible; it is the presenter's observation about what is happening in the situation.

A second general rule for uncovering indirect resistance involves not talking for a couple of moments after the presenter has stated what he or she has observed. There may be a temptation to elaborate on the observation, or to support it with evidence. However, continuing the statement will reduce the tension in the situation. Without tension, the person who is resisting feels no discomfort, and is unlikely to address the issue directly. Moreover, elaborating on the original statement may increase the other person's defensiveness and reduce the chances of solving the problem.

If stating the problem in direct, non-punishing terms fails to bring the resistance out into the open, there may be little more the audit team can do to overcome the indirect resistance. The best strategy in this case is to avoid resisting the resistance. Team members should support the person who is resisting and proceed with the implementation of recommendations as far as possible.

Building an Ongoing Audit Programme

As the pace of change increases, and as organisation leaders become more and more committed to improving their effectiveness and efficiency, audits of all types of processes will become more common. The most effective companies will establish programmes of ongoing audits, whereby a number of goals can be accomplished:

- Performance improvements can be measured over time.
- Important changes in the company's environment can be systematically monitored.
- Managers can make a habit of change and improvement, rather than resisting it.
- Those areas that are of highest importance to the company can be routinely improved.
- Processes can be modified to be in alignment with changes in strategy or in the environment.

As with all management techniques, however, an enduring programme of ongoing audits requires that audits become integrated into the overall management system. The following guidelines are keys to weaving audits into the fabric of day-to-day operations.

Establish Support for Ongoing Audits

While support for audits begins at the executive level, ownership for the audit process must be felt throughout the organisation if an ongoing programme is to be successful. The following actions will help to broaden support for the audit process, while ensuring greater benefit from the audit.

- *Share the results of the audit with everyone throughout the organisation.*

By keeping others informed about the results of an audit, managers reassure those who participate in, and are affected by, the audit of the integrity of the process. Employees sometimes become suspicious of probing investigators; they may have doubts about how the information will be used, or even whether the information will be used at all. By sharing audit results, managers make an implicit commitment to improving the processes that have been evaluated.

- *Act on the audit results.*

Questions will be raised about continuing audits if early assessments bear no fruits. Failing to act on performance gaps that have been identified will lead to cynicism and lack of trust among those who work with the problems daily. On the other hand, improving a process can create the momentum that comes from accomplishment. Committing resources and attention to the improvement opportunities revealed by an audit also shows management commitment to the improvement process.

- *Let others know when performance has improved.*

Communicating the positive results from an audit is one way of rewarding the people who contributed to that improvement. It also builds faith in the effectiveness of the audit process. Moreover, showing that performance has improved is another means of reassuring people of a commitment to the improvement process.

- *Reward people for their part in improvements.*

Increasing efficiency and effectiveness can often be a threatening experience for those who are involved in a work process. Improving the way resources are used often means eliminating the need for some of the people who have been involved in the process. Although flatter, leaner organisations often preclude the possibility of offering promotions, managers should nevertheless attempt to ensure that people who contribute to performance improvement find their own situations better rather than worse as a result.

Rewards for helping to close performance gaps may span a range from thanking people for their efforts to planning a group celebration to offering bonuses or pay increases for improvement. Rewards are especially meaningful when people are allowed to suggest what rewards they would like for their contribution. This may provide managers with new ideas for rewards that may be less costly to the organisation than financial recognition.

- *Involve a wide variety of people in the audit process.*

People can be involved in the audit process in many ways. By involving people from a broad spectrum, more people learn about audit techniques and results, thus spreading commitment to the audit process throughout the organisation. By involving many people in the data-gathering process, employees feel that action plans growing out of the audit were a result of their input. Excluding people from the data-gathering phase usually reduces the feeling of ownership for the results, thus making people feel as if initiatives are being imposed on them. By the same token, involving a broad range of people in the development of action plans expands ownership for the plans and allows for the generation of more ideas.

Part 3

Implementing a Cost of Quality Audit: Questions and Checklists

This part of the Cost of Quality Audit comprises a series of questions based on the fourteen steps given in Part 1. These questions have been designed to help you plan and implement your audit in a straightforward and practical manner, covering all the relevant parts of the audit in the right order.

Nevertheless, every business and every organisation is different and there will be areas of this audit that require more, less or no attention in your own case (for example, the conduct of the audit will be influenced by how well mapped and understood your core processes are, etc). For that reason, these questions are all designed to be adapted and amended to suit your particular needs. If a question doesn't make sense in your organisation, change it; if team members (or interviewees) suggest a better version of the question, use it!

To recap, there are fourteen steps in a Cost of Quality Audit.

- Step 1 Choosing the Supervisory Team
- Step 2 Choosing the Processes to be Audited
- Step 3 Communicating the Audit Plan
- Step 4 Choosing the Audit Teams
- Step 5 Defining Training Needs and Setting a Schedule
- Step 6 Defining and Mapping the Business Process
- Step 7 Preparing to Calculate Quality Costs
- Step 8 Determining the Causes of Quality Costs
- Step 9 Interviewing Staff
- Step 10 Allocating Costs
- Step 11 Preparing the Audit Report
- Step 12 Preparing the Combined Audit Report
- Step 13 Sharing the Findings and Taking Action

- Step 14 Developing a Continuing Cycle of Audit and Improvement

Note: Before you answer the questions and complete the checklists that follow, you may like to refer to the *Introduction*, which will give you a comprehensive insight into the Cost of Quality along with an explanation of some of the terms used. You may also like to refer to the section that follows Step 14, entitled *Avoiding the Pitfalls of a Cost of Quality Audit*, plus *Appendix A* and *Appendix B*. Additionally, useful background information is given for each step before the questions themselves are listed.

Step 1

Choosing the Supervisory Team

BACKGROUND INFORMATION

Applying simple rules to the selection of supervisory team members can make the difference between an unimaginative financial report and one that identifies clear and profitable ways forward for the company. Three members should be selected for the audit team.

1. The team leader.
2. A senior member of the finance or accounts department.
3. A member of the training/personnel/human resources team or a senior administrative assistant.

The questions below have been compiled to help ensure that this happens.

QUESTIONS

The audit process

- How will individual business processes be identified and assessed?
  Note: The organisation should not be audited as a whole.
- Is it understood that in a large organisation this may mean conducting as many as 30 separate Cost of Quality assessments?
- How will consistency across all these assessments be ensured?
- In order to achieve this, will key supervisory team members be involved in the preparation and conduct of each of the audits?
  Note: In a large organisation, it will be unreasonably time-consuming for team members to be involved at every stage of each assessment.
- Who will oversee the creation of the supervisory team?

1. The Team Leader

Is there a Total Quality manager or director, or a Business Improvement manager or Director in your organisation? If so, will they lead the team? If not, who is responsible for that function in your organisation? If there is more than one person, on what criteria will the leader be chosen?

- Will the team leader's seniority reflect the importance that the company attaches to the results of this audit?
- Will the team leader demonstrate top management commitment to the project?
- Will the team leader have the experience and ability to think widely about issues across the whole company?
- Will the team leader be able to insist on attention to detail, without becoming immersed in the minutiae of each assessment?

2. A Senior Member of the Finance or Accounts Department

- Will the senior member of the finance or accounts department be able to ensure that consistent measures are used in each assessment?
- How will the senior member of the finance or accounts department ensure that the dangers of double-counting are minimised?

Note: The presence of the accountant on the team is a reminder that the Cost of Quality Audit is, in part, a genuine financial audit.

3. A Member of the Training/Personnel/HR team or a senior administrative assistant

- Will this team member be closely involved with all aspects of the company's work?
- Will this team member know many of the individuals on each audit team?
- Will this team member be made responsible for training the members of each audit team or will that be delegated to audit team leaders?
- Will this team member ensure that each audit team keeps to established schedules or will that be delegated to audit team leaders?
- Will this team member ensure that each assessment team produces the required report in an appropriate format or will that be delegated to audit team leaders?

Note: The selection of assessment teams is covered in Step 4 of the section *Steps in a Cost of Quality Audit.*

Now that members of the supervisory team have been selected, the next task is to choose the processes that need to be audited. The questions that follow, which relate to Step 2, will help you to do this.

Step 2

CHOOSING THE PROCESS TO BE AUDITED

BACKGROUND INFORMATION

Understanding and selecting appropriate business processes is a key element in a successful audit. The audit team must identify a range of processes to be assessed, limiting the number of processes and the extent of each process according to the skills and time available.

The questions below will help to achieve this task.

QUESTIONS

- Has the supervisory team decided on the scope of the Cost of Quality Audit?
- Has this task been undertaken in conjunction with the CEO or the management team as a whole?

Note: The role of the audit will not normally be to come up with a definitive statement of Quality costs across the whole organisation (see Figure 3 and relevant text in the Introduction).

- One purpose of the audit will be to focus attention on the company's core business processes. Have these processes been identified and mapped? When? Is the data up to date? How do you know?

Note: Those that have not done so will find the Cost of Quality Audit doubly valuable because of the additional insights into the working of the company that will be found.

- To ensure that the Cost of Quality Audit is taken seriously by staff and managers, processes should be chosen which, together, touch or cross every single site, department, operation or team in the organisation. How will you choose the processes to be audited? How far will expected outcomes affect the processes you choose? Will you give priority to processes thought to be inefficient or wasteful? Or to processes that are easy to audit?
- Will most of the processes chosen be those that end with the customer?
- Will the processes also include internal ones such as:

◊ choosing, ordering and distributing stationery

◊ identifying staffing requirements

◊ advertising

◊ interviewing and appointing new members of staff?

Note: The objective of including every department and significant work group will define how many processes are chosen for assessment.

- If a large number of processes is identified, will it be appropriate to make the first round of assessments a pilot scheme and restrict the audit to one site or division?
- If the company is unfamiliar with business process management, will it be appropriate to limit the scope of the first audit?
- In the long run, will it be more effective to set limited, but achievable, targets for the audit?
- How might you limit the scope of individual processes to manageable proportions?

Note: You may wish to refer to the example of the restaurant in Step 2 of the section *Steps in a Cost of Quality Audit.*

- Will the supervisory or the audit team define the starting-point and finishing-point for each business process to be assessed?
- How will you establish boundaries between the supervisory team and the audit teams?
- Will individual audit teams be given complete freedom to decide what tasks to include in the process?

Note: Almost invariably, it will be found that the scope of the process and the "inputs" considered will increase as the audit team continues its work. For further information on assessment teams, see Step 4.

Having identified the business processes to be assessed, the next step is communicating the audit plan. The checklist that follows, which relates to Step 3, will help you to do this.

Step 3

COMMUNICATING THE AUDIT PLAN

BACKGROUND INFORMATION

The supervisory team must establish its objectives and develop an appropriate mission statement. By effectively communicating its intentions, the team will help to allay fears and win enthusiastic cooperation.

The checklist below will help a team to ascertain the following.

1. The audit team's intentions in conducting the audit.
2. What the mission statement will include.
3. The purposes of the mission statement.

CHECKLIST

1. The Supervisory Team's Intentions in Conducting the Audit

- Is the team absolutely clear in what it wishes to achieve in conducting the audit?
- How did it decide?
- Condense the aim into an audit mission statement that encapsulates the chief purposes of the audit.

2. What the Mission Statement will Include

- Include references that the team wishes to:

  ◊ better understand the key business processes which drive the organisation's performance and profitability.

  ◊ identify specific Quality improvement projects which will rapidly deliver tangible benefits to the company and its staff.

- Include reference to the intention - within the processes being assessed - to identify and reduce waste, rework and the cost of product failure and service breakdown, wherever they are found.
- Ensure that these terms are widely understood within the organisation?

- Ensure that staff understand that, by cutting down on waste, rework and failure, they will be able to concentrate on more productive, rewarding and enjoyable work.
- Include an undertaking that no blame will be attached to any individual for costs uncovered by the audit.

Note: You may like to refer to Figure 5, which outlines how to overcome resistance to Cost of Quality auditing.

- Include, if possible, an undertaking that no jobs will be lost as a result of any savings that may be made following the audit and its recommendations.

Note: Once again, Figure 5 shows some useful information for dealing with this scenario.

3. The Purposes of the Mission Statement

- Present the mission statement to the Board of Directors or the senior management team to help clarify the team's intentions and the results that can be expected for the audit.
- Refer to the mission statement when briefing audit teams and in preparing the final report.
- Use the mission statement as the basis for all staff and assessment team briefings to ensure a consistency of purpose and to help clear up potential misunderstandings.

Having established the contents of the audit plan and the best way to communicate it, the next step is to choose the audit teams. The questions below, which relate to Step 4, will help you to do this.

Step 4

Choosing the Audit Teams

BACKGROUND INFORMATION

The supervisory team should now select members of each audit team, looking for people with the skills and experience to understand each business process well. The work of these teams will ultimately decide the success of the whole audit.

The questions below offer some guidance.

QUESTIONS

- How will you balance the need to minimise disruption and to complete the audits as quickly as possible?
- How many teams will you choose?
- Will each department be represented on the assessment team?
- Will you involve the audit team leader in the selection of other team members? Or will each audit team elect its own leader?
- Does each audit team member have a good understanding of the process involved?
- Can it be ensured that each audit team member does not have obvious vested interests in maintaining the status quo?

Note: For example, a key department manager may be reluctant to reveal waste or inefficiency for fear that this may put promotion opportunities at risk.

- Might younger department members be the most suitable? If so, will they have the authority to interview people effectively?

Note: However, they should still have been with the company for at least two years in order to be familiar with its operation overall.

- At this point, will individual department managers or team leaders be asked to nominate an enthusiastic and communicative member of staff to represent them on the audit team?
- Depending on the make-up of each audit team, will it be helpful to

nominate a different member of the finance or accounts department to sit on each team?

Note: This will help to minimise the time needed to train non-financial staff in the fundamentals of accounting. It will also help to avoid audit teams spending valuable time measuring or calculating costs that may already be well known to the accounts or finance department.

- If the number of individual Cost of Quality audits to be run is very few, will the supervisory team remain closely involved at almost every stage of the audit? Or will it allow the audit teams more latitude?
- If the number is large, what will the supervisory team be responsible for?

Once members for each of the audit teams have been chosen, the next step in the audit is to define training needs and set a schedule. The questions below, which relate to Step 5, will help you to do this.

Step 5

Defining Training/Development Needs and Setting a Schedule

BACKGROUND INFORMATION

Not every organisation will need additional training in process management or quality measures. For those that do, it is a straightforward process that will offer substantial advantages long after the audit has been completed.

The questions below will help you to ascertain your own training needs.

QUESTIONS

Training Outline

- Once the mission statement has been agreed and the process audit teams have been chosen, how will the supervisory team identify learning and development needs of audit team members?
- Or will that responsibility be delegated to the audit team leaders or to the team members themselves?
- If further training and development is provided, how will you test the application of the concepts learned?
- Will the above focus on applying the general rules to the specific conditions of the organisation or process under discussion?
- Will one of the key components of training be a proper understanding of the concept of the internal customer?

Note: Assessment team members may easily overlook Quality costs if they focus only on the requirements of the end user of the product or service.

Clarifying Training Needs

- To help clarify training needs, how will you ensure that a consistent message is communicated to all assessment teams?
- To help clarify training needs, how will you ensure that the demands placed on these teams are reasonable?

The Supervisory Team's Role

- Will the supervisory team conduct a limited Cost of Quality audit itself?

Note: This may be advisable, and if undertaken should be confined to an internal process that is well-known to all the team members and which does not require the involvement of other staff.

- Would identifying and providing training, or hiring new employees be suitable processes for the preliminary audit referred to in the previous question?

Note: The results of this "demonstration audit" need not be published. The purpose of conducting the audit is to familiarise the supervisory team with some of the problems that will subsequently be faced by the audit teams.

- Having defined the mission statement and agreed training needs, how will the supervisory team agree a schedule?
- Will all the assessments be run concurrently?
- What degree of control over the audit process will be exercised by the supervisory team?
- Will the supervisory team decide how often the audit teams should report their progress?
- Will the supervisory team agree a structure for the final report to be submitted by each audit team?

Note: Step 11 in the section *Steps in a Cost of Quality Audit* gives details on preparing the audit report.

Briefing Staff

- How and when will the whole audit scheme be presented to the company?
- Will all members of staff be briefed, even those who will not directly be involved in any of the assessments?

Note: It is important that all members are briefed. It will help to avoid misguided rumours spreading about the intentions of the audit team.

- In a large organisation, will this briefing be undertaken via individual managers, who will need to be fully briefed first or handled centrally?
- How will top-management involvement and support be communicated to staff?
- How will you explain that a Cost of Quality Audit is quite unlike a standard financial audit?

- Have you got the tools to explain to staff that the Cost of Quality audit is designed to give everyone involved a completely new picture of the organisation?

Note: The audit will reveal dramatic and unexpected statistics but, at the same time, uncover opportunities for the company to revolutionise the whole way it does business.

- How much briefing will audit team members be given on typical Cost of Quality audit results? Will too much data encourage them to feel they have to reach a magic target in order to demonstrate that their audit has been a successful one?

Having established training needs, the next step is to define and map the business process. The checklist that follows, which relates to Step 6, will help you to do this.

Step 6

DEFINING AND MAPPING THE BUSINESS PROCESS

BACKGROUND INFORMATION

Here, individual assessment teams lay the groundwork for their cost assessment, developing a clearer understanding of the process that they are auditing.

The checklist below will help you to follow this through in the correct sequence in order to produce a process flow map.

CHECKLIST

- Establish what data is already available to the audit team on the process it is going to audit.
- Establish whether process mapping training or software is required.
- Ensure that all audit team members are familiar with every stage of the process.

Note: At this stage, the intention should be to make the process definition as comprehensive as possible. The sample process flow map shown in Figure 6 shows the use of conventional mapping symbols. Figure 7 shows how the map can be abbreviated.

- Verify the accuracy of the new or existing process map.
- Ensure that the supervisory team compares the maps submitted by each audit team to ensure that there is no overlap between the different processes being assessed.
- Ensure that the audit team retains a copy of the fuller version process map for the audit itself.

Note: Many of the potential Quality costs will inevitably lie in those areas of the map that have been left out. The fuller map should also remain an essential source of reference in all future assessments in the Cost of Quality audit cycle.

Now that full and abbreviated versions of the process flow map have been produced and distributed, the next step is to prepare to calculate Quality costs. The questions below, which relate to Step 7, will help you to do this.

Step 7

PREPARING TO CALCULATE QUALITY COSTS

BACKGROUND INFORMATION

The audit teams should now begin to gather available data from in-house sources, which will help them allocate realistic costs within the main Quality cost categories.

The questions below will help your assessment teams to do this.

QUESTIONS

- As preparation for the analysis of time-related costs, does the audit team have a list of all the staff involved in any way at every stage of the process? Or will it prepare one?

Note: Additional staff members may be identified as involved in the process during Step 9 of Part 1. They can simply be added to the list at that time.

- How will staff be categorised in terms of wage/salary? Will two or three bands be enough?

Note: This framework will be used to convert time spent on Quality-related activities into cash amounts.

- Will the audit team, with input from the accounts department representative, calculate the average burden rate for each group of employees in terms of one percentage figure for all employees? Or will it be described as two different figures if there is a significantly different burden rate for the highest paid people in the organisation as compared to the lower paid?

Note: The burden rate usually runs between 15 and 30% of wages.

The next step is for the audit team to break down Quality costs into time-related costs, "out-of-pocket" costs relating to materials and supplies, and other intangible costs. The checklist that follows, which relates to Step 8, will help you to achieve this.

Step 8

DETERMINING THE CAUSES OF QUALITY COSTS

BACKGROUND INFORMATION

The assessment here uses brainstorming techniques to determine bottlenecks and other sources of waste, delay and rework with the business process in question. The brainstorming workshop should be structured in four phases.

The checklist below relates to the preparation for these workshops, then each of the four phases.

CHECKLIST

Preparing for the Brainstorming Workshop

- Does the audit team have the necessary brainstorming skills and experience? Is further training and development required?
- How will the team introduce and teach the idea of prevention, appraisal and failure costs to participants?

Note: The terms "Prevention", "Appraisal" and "Failure" are further defined in the Introduction.

- If necessary, the audit team should call in additional members of staff to join the brainstorming session.

Note: Involving other staff members at this stage has been shown to be an effective way of winning the support of employees who are otherwise sceptical or critical of the audit.

The tasks and questions that follow relate to the structure in four phases of the brainstorming workshop.

Phase 1

- Before the workshop, create a condensed process self-assessment form with a copy of the process map and a short definition of the terms prevention, appraisal and failure attached to the form.

Note: Refer to Figure 8 in Step 8 of the section *Steps in a Cost of Quality Audit,* which shows this form. No attempt should be made at this stage to attach any cost estimates to the activities that are identified.

Phase 2

- At the workshop, invite participants to take turns to call out one activity from their worksheet and write it up in the appropriate category.
- In the event of duplication, write up the activity twice and combine the two listings later. Try not to exclude any activities that are called out at this stage.
- Invite participants to contribute new suggestions as a result of hearing the activities that others have identified. Write these up also.

Note: At this stage, no discussion or evaluation of any of the activities should be allowed.

Phase 3

- In this phase of the workshop, group and order the suggested areas and activities into Prevention, Appraisal, Internal Failure and External Failure costs, amending or removing any that are generally agreed to be inappropriate or irrelevant.
- Ensure that built-in costs are not overlooked.

Note: Built-in costs are often called "yield allowances."

- Produce a listing, similar in scope to that shown in Appendix A but "personalised" to suit the business process under discussion.

Phase 4

- Invite participants to consider the Cost of Quality factors that they have identified in another way.

Within each of the four categories - Prevention, Appraisal, Internal Failure, External Failure - costs will be found to fall into:

◊ tangible or out-of-pocket expenses

◊ time

◊ other intangible costs.

Tangible or Out-of-Pocket Expenses

- If your company operates a manufacturing process, check that these expenses include:

◊ raw materials or parts which are rejected, damaged, or otherwise not used.

◊ finished and part finished goods which are thrown away because they do not conform to requirements in some way.

- For service or administrative processes, check that these expenses include:

  ◊ printed materials, stationery, and other outputs, which cannot be used.

  ◊ goods and services which have been ordered in error or in excess and which are, therefore, wasted or not used.

Note: Out-of-pocket expenses will also include all other measurable costs relating to:

◊ warranties

◊ refunds

◊ safety materials, and so on.

Time

- Remember to include time spent working on or with goods and services that are wasted and never used and working on:

  ◊ putting things right

  ◊ correcting damage

  ◊ repairing damage

  ◊ errors

  ◊ product failures

  ◊ service failures.

- Also include time spent "rebuilding" relationships with customers that have been damaged as a result of delay or the provision of faulty goods and services.

Other Intangible Costs

- These costs should principally include "opportunity costs".

Note: These are one of the most contentious areas of Quality Costing. They relate almost exclusively to external failure. Appendix B shows the categories of Internal and External Failure allocated as tangible, time-related and intangible.

- Remember to include the cost of alienating customers and so losing:

  ◊ their future custom

  ◊ the custom of associated companies

◊ the custom of their families and friends

- Also include the cost of sales, marketing and promotion to replace a lost customer.

Note: The final refinement of the different elements of the Cost of Quality is shown in Figure 9.

Having planned how to use the brainstorming workshop to identify and categorise potential Quality-related costs associated with the process under review, the next step is to interview staff. The checklist below, which relates to Step 9, will help you to do this.

Step 9

INTERVIEWING STAFF

BACKGROUND INFORMATION

Each audit team member should brief and interview those involved in the process to get their input on likely and unsuspected Quality costs.

The questions below will help you to:

- prepare for interviewing
- understand the five stages of interviewing
- recognise the problems at interview stage.

CHECKLIST

Preparing for the Interview

- Agree an interviewing procedure and schedule in order to gather the necessary information.
- Decide whether all staff associated with the process can be interviewed.
- If not, identify appropriate representatives from each department or work group who could be interviewed.

Note: It may be helpful in some cases to interview a small group of three or four staff. This group approach will be helpful if the interviewer does not have a close working knowledge of the process stage that is "in the spotlight."

- Consider interviewing a small group rather than individuals so that interviewees can give each other ideas and provoke lateral thinking on possible Quality costs and allow cross checking of each other's estimates of time spent on particular activities.

Note: Depending on the number of issues to be covered and the number of people present, the interview may last from one to three hours.

The next section relates to the five stages of interviewing.

Phase 1

- Give a brief explanation of the aims of the interview and the terms being used.

Note: It is not necessary for the interviewee to understand the fine distinctions between different categories of Quality costs. The interviewer will be responsible for allocating costs to the relevant category.

- During this explanation, give examples of the sort of costs that are being identified.

Note: Figure 2 and Appendix A give examples of these.

Phase 2

- Ask interviewees to describe the major and minor functions of their:
  - ◊ job
  - ◊ department
  - ◊ work group

Note: These comments can be recorded on a simple job function survey, as shown in Figure 10.

Phase 3

- Identify the number of people in the department/work group and agree on how many fall into each of the three or four salary levels in Step 7.
- Record this information and use it to convert time spent on Quality-related issues into a financial equivalent.

Phase 4

For each of the major activities identified in Phase 2, go through the list of causes identified by the assessment team in Step 8 and illustrated in Appendix B.

- Ask interviewees to estimate:
  - ◊ the amounts of services and materials (tangible costs) associated with each item
  - ◊ the time spent by different people in the department on various activities
- For each estimate, record the period to which it relates (day, week, month and so on).

Note: The periods quoted do not need to be consistent, but must be known so that the subsequent financial calculation can be made accurately.

- Now record these answers on a Cost of Quality survey sheet.

Note: For an example of one of these, refer to Figure 10.

- Ask the interviewees to break down the time estimate into the salary levels already agreed, in order to allow an accurate conversion into financial cost.
- Throughout the interview, invite and record comments from the interviewees about the reasons why large blocks of time are spent on Quality-related activities.

Note: These areas will suggest ideas for improvement projects in the analysis phase of the audit.

Phase 5

- Encourage interviewees to think of as many other Prevention and Appraisal activities as possible, as well as other causes of failure and rework, apart from those listed.
- Ask for tangible and time-related costs for each new activity identified.

Problems at the interview stage

- Are interviewees uncertain about how much time should be spent on a particular activity?

  ◊ Discuss the activity until a rough estimate can be made.

- Are interviewees afraid to reveal figures that could suggest incompetence or complacency on their part or on the part of their manager?

  ◊ Reassure interviewees by telling them figures that have been found in other (unnamed) departments and by reminding them that no blame will be attached to the individual, however high the cost of wasted time or materials that they report.

- Are interviewees offering exaggerated estimates in order to highlight incompetence that they perceive in their managers or in company systems?

  ◊ Look for signs of aggression or hostility in the interviewee's answers and double-check their answers with others in the department.

- Are interviewees confused by the division of costs into Prevention, Appraisal and Failure?

  ◊ This is not important. The interviewer or audit team can subsequently reorder activities as appropriate.

Having conducted all the interviews, the next stage in the audit is to allocate costs. The checklist that follows, which relates to Step 10, will help you to do this.

Step 10

ALLOCATING COSTS

BACKGROUND INFORMATION

The audit team should now use agreed formulas and the information derived from interviews and management reports to allocate financial costs within each of the four main categories.

The checklist below will help you to make these allocations.

CHECKLIST

- Once all interviews have been completed, the audit team should begin to allocate costs to each of the activities that has been identified.
- The finance/accounts representative should identify any areas where costs have already been calculated or are available.
- These are likely to include:

  ◊ payroll breakdowns

  ◊ production expense or scrap report

  ◊ travel expenses claims

  ◊ repair and replacement cost reports.
- Obtain and divide costs between normal activity and Quality-related activity. (If necessary, interview a department manager for suggestions on how to make this apportionment).
- Do not overlook other reports or management information sources which may record how often a failure occurs or an assessment activity occurs.

Note: It will be quicker and easier to deduce Cost of Quality figures from this information than to try to collect the information afresh.

- Using their interview results, the audit team should now arrive at estimates for each activity and annualise those costs in all cases.

Note: It is essential to pay particular attention to any special seasonal considerations which may distort figures in any given period.

- The audit team should now use data from the accounts department, as well as the salary bands and burden rates identified in Step 6 to convert these raw figures into monetary terms.
- Remember to make allowance for intangible or "opportunity" costs, which were not touched on in the interviews.
- Since this is the most difficult area to define, and because of the potential for double-counting, the supervisory team may want to call together all the audit teams to agree a common standard for arriving at intangible costs.

Note: This standard will vary widely from business to business and from sector to sector. You might also like to refer to the information on opportunity costs under the subhead "Other intangible costs" in Step 8.

Once all the interviews are complete, and all the additional information has been collected, the audit team should begin to prepare the audit report. The checklist below, which relates to Step 11, will help you to do this.

Step 11

PREPARING THE AUDIT REPORT

BACKGROUND INFORMATION

The audit reports should condense and summarise the cost information that has been gathered, presenting the supervisory team with consistent data on which they can base their own conclusions.

QUESTIONS

- Use the main part of the report to describe and illustrate the process under assessment, paying attention to any areas where the process was truncated.

Note: You may like to refer to Step 6, where this process was discussed.

- Then present an assessment of costs, presented as they have been calculated.
- Clearly identify the process under examination and account for the costs by the four categories of Prevention, Appraisal, Internal Failure and External Failure.
- Show the percentage and currency value of tangible out-of-pocket expenses allocated to each of the four Quality categories.
- Show the percentage of staff time allocated to Quality costs and its monetary value for each Quality category.
- Show the currency value of intangible "opportunity" costs.
- Combine these costs to present a total Cost of Quality for the process, broken down into the four Quality categories.
- Describe the key sources of substantial costs, noting any process components identified by the audit team as contributing substantially to Quality costs.
- Make note of any reservations or qualifications that may apply to the figures.
- Make recommendations for future assessments or for action based on the assessment results with which the whole team agrees.
- Prepare a detailed breakdown of all Quality costs, including spreadsheet

data, interview results and notes on assumptions, as an appendix to the audit report.

Note: An example of spreadsheet information is given in Figure 11.

- Note any problems or concerns encountered during the audit in the appendix.
- When submitting the report, the audit team must retain copies of all working papers and documents which may be needed to justify the figures or for future audits.

Having prepared the audit report, it is now time to look at preparation of the combined audit report. The checklist below, which relates to Step 12, will help you to do this.

Step 12

Preparing the Combined Audit Report

BACKGROUND INFORMATION

The audit team is now in a position to prepare a combined Cost of Quality report which brings together the results of each audit and focuses on opportunities for process improvement and cost reduction.

The checklist below will help you to make decisions about each of the areas mentioned.

1. Allocating responsibility for improvement.
2. Opportunities for improvement.
3. The contents of the Combined Audit Report.

CHECKLIST

Initial Preparation

- Each member of the audit team should read all the audit reports.
- Audit team representatives can be called in for further clarification of any of the figures and conclusions that have been presented.
- Before writing the report, the audit team should refer again to the mission statement and consider the following points:

1. Allocating Responsibility for Improvement

- Approach Cost of Quality reduction as a self-improvement exercise.

Note: It will be salutary for the audit team and for all senior management to accept responsibility themselves for the costs that have been uncovered.

- Consider how processes can be better managed to prevent Quality costs occurring.
- Consider how to invest in staff so they are better equipped to find solutions.

Note: The costs of training and restructuring are all, of course, prevention costs.

- Think about staff empowerment and whether the initial Cost of Quality audits will have gone some way towards creating a sense of empowerment.
- Consider whether imposing change will work. If staff suggest and adopt change, is it more likely to work?
- Avoid being too prescriptive.
- Remember that responsibility must be handed back to the audit teams and to staff working on each business process.

2. Opportunities for Improvement

- The team must at least consider:
  - ◊ paying more to hire or retain qualified and experienced staff
  - ◊ encouraging and sharing the cost of continuing education for employees
  - ◊ increasing the level of targeted internal training
  - ◊ developing coordinated Quality improvement initiatives with key suppliers?

Note: All of these opportunities should deliver consequential savings in Failure costs.

3. The Contents of the Audit Report

- The audit report must include a concise summary of the relevant Cost of Quality statistics and a statement of intent.
- The summary of statistics must be presented graphically in a way that is clear to all members of staff.
- The statement of intent must:
  - ◊ accept responsibility for the costs identified
  - ◊ outline improvement opportunities
  - ◊ state the management's willingness to fund investment in cost reduction
  - ◊ hand back responsibility for delivery improvement to the staff involved.

Note: For information relating to a statement of intent, refer to Step 12.

The penultimate step in this audit is about sharing findings and taking action. The checklist below, which relates to Step 13, will help you to do this.

Step 13

SHARING THE FINDINGS AND TAKING ACTION

BACKGROUND INFORMATION

The combined audit report should now be presented to senior management and to all company staff as soon as possible. Top management must accept responsibility for problems that have caused Quality-related costs, but empower staff to identify ways of reducing these costs.

The checklist below will allow this process to happen.

CHECKLIST

- The report should be presented first to the CEO and senior management team, then to the company as a whole.
- It should be undertaken either by the audit team or by the managers who briefed the company at Step 5.
- The presentation to the CEO and senior management team should lead to serious questioning of the report's assumptions and to a reappraisal of the company's overall business strategy and performance.
- The supervisory team must be prepared to answer questions about the possibility of integrating the Cost of Quality measures into a company-wide improvement programme.
- The presentation to staff should be done as soon as possible.

Note: The interviews will have generated considerable interest among staff and the audit team needs to capitalise on that enthusiasm in moving forward to seek cost improvements.

- The presentation should follow the same approach as the report itself, highlighting key costs and focusing on the role of staff in identifying and implementing process improvements.
- Management and staff should be reminded that:

  ◊ the costs identified in the audit are not definitive

  ◊ a number of significant costs may have been overlooked

◊ the audit only relates to certain core processes.

- Staff should be encouraged to identify and report new factors contributing to the Cost of Quality in their area.
- Staff should be encouraged to suggest ways in which those costs could be addressed.
- At the presentation, the audit teams will be asked to develop specific recommendations for improving the process on which they were working.
- These recommendations must be developed in conjunction with the process staff that the audit team interviewed during the assessments.
- These recommendations should be presented in less than one month.

Note: Just as the audit report must not prescribe solutions, so the presentation must also be careful not to do so.

- The supervisory team should look for common themes in the improvement suggestions that are made, so the whole organisation can begin to benefit from the best ideas that are being applied to specific processes.
- In all cases, the supervisory and audit teams must credit fully the staff who initially developed these "bandwagon" suggestions.

The Cost of Quality improvement initiative started in this step should immediately begin to drive future audits. The final step in this audit is about developing a continuing cycle of audit and improvement. The checklist that follows, which relates to Step 14, will help you to ensure this happens.

Step 14

DEVELOPING A CONTINUING CYCLE OF AUDIT AND IMPROVEMENT

BACKGROUND INFORMATION

The success of the Cost of Quality Audit depends entirely on the extent to which it is just the first step in an ongoing cycle of assessment, measurement and Quality improvement.

The checklist below will help you to keep the cycle going.

CHECKLIST

- Use the Cost of Quality improvement initiative immediately to drive future audits.
- The supervisory and audit teams as well as individual process teams should seek confirmation that the changes being made are delivering real improvements and cost savings.
- The initiative will be helped by the support and commitment of top management.
- The supervisory and audit teams should display Cost of Quality measures and improvement targets and results publicly and prominently.
- As a general rule, individual processes should be assessed at least every six months.

Appendix A: Cost Analysis

The following listing will help in identifying and allocating different Quality costs. For most categories, examples of typical costs are included. The listing is not intended to be comprehensive, and every organisation can, and must, add to it.

Prevention costs — the cost of trying to prevent things going wrong — can be further broken down into:

Customer assessment

— customer assessment/surveys

— analysis of competitors

Product or service design

— design reviews/field trials

— design qualification/stress tests

Acquisition of inputs or supplies

— supplier reviews/rating

— purchase order reviews

— supplier quality planning

Operations

— process control and planning

— job training

— preventive maintenance

— test equipment/software design

— control and monitoring staff, equipment and software

Human Resources

— training courses, materials and equipment

— safety equipment

— training and Quality rewards and recognition costs

— staff selection/orientation/training

— exit interviews

— succession planning

Information systems

— verification of input data

— contingency planning

— information system testing

— preventative software (like spell checkers)

— data back-up costs

Quality administration

— salaries/expenses for Quality assurance of products/services

— Quality programme planning and performance reporting

General management

— contingency planning

— rewards/training process design

Appraisal costs — the cost of checking to see if things have gone wrong — can be further broken down into:

Supplier appraisal costs

— receiving or incoming inspections/tests

— source inspection and control programmes (time at supplier's site)

— qualification of supplier's product

Operations

— outside endorsement and certification of products and services

— measurement and inspection equipment and software

— planned inspections, tests, audits

— product or service quality audits

— equipment/task set-up inspections

— outside endorsements and certifications of products or services

— report checking

— process control measurements

External appraisal costs

— field performance evaluation of products or services

Review of test and inspection data

Testing and inspection efforts in all support functions

Information systems

— hardware and software for inspection and testing

Internal failure costs — the cost of things going wrong which do not directly affect the customer — can be further broken down into:

Customer requirements

— stocking surplus products or retaining additional staff

— premium transport/delivery costs

— rework due to incorrect understanding or acceptance of needs/requirements

— overtime, costs associated with the urgent provision of a service

Product or service design failure costs

— redesign

— rework due to design changes

Acquisition failure

— unusable supply losses (including information reacquisition cost)

— premium transport/delivery costs

— stocking surplus supplies

— time spent on supplies replacement (due to rejects)

— supplier corrective action efforts

— rework of supplier rejects

Design

— scrap/inventory write-offs due to design/service changes

Operations

— equipment breakdown repair costs

— excess equipment/staff

— scrap due to operations

— expediting

— trouble shooting or failure analysis

— rework and reinspection

— time lost due to equipment failure

— excessive set-up/changeover time

— time lost due to safety problems

Financial management

— financial write-offs

— loss on discounts not taken

— interest lost on uncontrolled receivables

— interest lost on invoice delays

— incorrect accounting entries

— excessive time to close the books

— invoice errors

Entire organisation

— penalties, fines, legal settlements

— excess absenteeism

— excess turnover

— faulty documentation

— mistakes in pricing and estimating

— schedule changes

— overtime

— administrative errors

— delays and bottlenecks

Information systems

— systems redundancy or excess equipment

— inadequate systems/hardware

— systems failures

— programme restarts

— output errors

— report reruns

Human resources

— worker compensation payments

External failure costs — the cost of things going wrong which directly affect the customer — can be further broken down into:

Complaint Investigations

Returned/rejected product/service costs

— refused product/service value/processing

— returned product transportation costs

Field problems

— travel to address problems

Recall activities and costs

Warranty/refund guarantee claim costs and processing

Liability costs or claims

Loss of customer goodwill

Cost of replacing lost customers

Credit memos and discounts for defective products and services

Environmental and regulatory compliance penalties

Appendix B: Cost Analysis Allocated to Cost Types

The following listing shows how the Quality costs identified as costs of Internal Failure and External Failure might be allocated as being either tangible, out-of-pocket expenses, or time-related expenses, or intangible "opportunity" costs. (See Step 8 for a full explanation).

	Tangible	*Time*	*Intangible*
Internal Failure costs:			
Customer requirements			
— stocking surplus products or retaining additional staff	x	x	
— premium transport/delivery costs	x		
— rework due to incorrect understanding or acceptance of needs/requirements		x	
— overtime, costs associated with the urgent provision of a service		x	
Product or service design failure costs			
— redesign		x	
— rework due to design changes		x	
Acquisition failure			
— unusable supply losses (including information reacquisition cost)	x		
— premium transport/delivery costs	x		
— stocking surplus supplies		x	
— time spent on supplies replacement (due to rejects)		x	
— supplier corrective action efforts		x	
— rework of supplier rejects		x	
Design			
— scrap/inventory write-offs due to design/service changes	x		
Operations			
— equipment breakdown repair costs	x		
— excess equipment/staff	x	x	
— scrap due to operations	x		
— expediting		x	
— trouble shooting or failure analysis		x	
— rework and reinspection		x	
— time lost due to equipment failure		x	
— excessive set-up/changeover time		x	
— time lost due to safety problems		x	
Financial management			
— financial write-offs	x		
— loss on discounts not taken	x		

— interest lost on uncontrolled receivables	x		
— interest lost on invoice delays	x		
— incorrect accounting entries		x	
— excessive time to close the books		x	
— invoice errors		x	
Entire organisation			
— penalties, fines, legal settlements	x		
— excess absenteeism	x		
— excess turnover	x		
— faulty documentation		x	
— mistakes in pricing and estimating	x	x	
— schedule changes	x	x	
— overtime	x	x	
— administrative errors	x	x	
— delays and bottlenecks	x	x	
Information systems			
— systems redundancy or excess equipment	x		
— inadequate systems/hardware	x	x	
— systems failures		x	
— programme restarts		x	
— output errors		x	
— report reruns		x	
Human resources			
— worker compensation payments	x	x	
External Failure costs:			
Complaint Investigations		x	
Returned/rejected product/service costs			
— refused product/service value/processing	x	x	x
— returned product transportation costs	x		
Field problems			
— travel to address problems	x	x	
Recall activities and costs	x	x	x
Warranty/refund guarantee claim costs and processing	x	x	
Liability costs or claims	x	x	x
Loss of customer goodwill			x
Cost of replacing lost customers	x	x	x
Credit memos and discounts for defective products and services		x	x
Environmental and regulatory compliance penalties	x	x	x

References, Bibliography and Useful Contacts

Publications

Bristow, Nigel and Sandberg, Sarah, *The Corporate Culture Audit*, Cambridge Strategy Publications, 2010

Crosby, Philip, *Quality is Free*, McGraw-Hill, 1979

Quality Digest ~ www.qualitydigest.com

Seddon, John, *Systems Thinking in the Public Sector*, Triarchy Press, 2008

University of Keele, *Internal Quality Audit Handbook*, www.keele.ac.uk, 2006

Wood, Douglas, *The Executive Guide to Understanding and Implementing Quality Cost Programs*, ASQ Quality Press, 2007

Groups and Associations

APQC: The American Productivity and Quality Center ~ www.apqc.org/

ASQ: The American Society for Quality ~ www.asq.org

Business Excellence ~ www.bexcellence.org

The EFQM Excellence Award ~ www.efqm.org

The Malcolm Baldrige Award ~ www.nist.gov/baldrige

The Quality Portal ~ http://thequalityportal.com

About the Author

At the time of writing, **W. Jeffery Howard** is a member of the APQC Consulting Group, a subsidiary of The American Productivity & Quality Center, Houston. Texas. He has led APQC projects in a variety of areas, including Baldrige assessment and implementation, ISO 9000, performance measurement, process design, simplification and improved effectiveness. He is a frequent instructor at APQC seminars and client courses.

About the Publisher

Whatever name you give it, your organisation is almost certainly looking for new ways to ♦ increase efficiency ♦ outsmart competitors ♦ win, delight and retain customers ♦ develop new products or services ♦ train, motivate and retain staff ♦ cut costs and delays ♦ increase profits.

Cambridge Strategy Publications has a highly-respected range of management resources to help you do exactly that. Now being used in more than 90 countries around the world, by private, public and governmental organisations large and small and in every business sector, CSP's non-financial, self-assessment audits will help you implement change fast.

Each of these 28 non-financial, company self-assessment audits is ready-to-run in your organisation and is available in print and as an e-audit.

Strategy & General Management

The Business Strategy Audit

The Business Innovation Audit

The Corporate Culture Audit

The Cost of Quality Audit

The Customer Satisfaction Audit

The Logistics Audit

The Organisational Leadership Audit

The Organisational Shadow-Side Audit

The Partnership and Alliances Audit

The Productivity Audit

The Technology Management Audit

Marketing

The Customer Loyalty Audit

The Customer Support Audit

The Franchising Audit

The Pricing Strategy Audit

The Strategic Marketing Plan Audit

Human Resources

The Employee Motivation Audit

The Human Resource Function Audit

The HR Information System Audit

The Human Resource Planning Audit

The Leadership Skills Audit

The Organisational Change Audit

The Payroll Audit

The People Policies Audit

The Performance Management Audit

The Reward and Benefits Audit

The Teams Audit

The Training and Development Audit

www.ingramcontent.com/pod-product-compliance
Lightning Source LLC
LaVergne TN
LVHW060212210926
848481LV00008B/2714